100

THINGS

MILLIONAIRES DO

LITTLE LESSONS IN CREATING WEALTH

D0809100

100

THINGS

MILLIONAIRES DO

LITTLE LESSONS IN CREATING WEALTH

NIGEL CUMBERLAND

First published in 2019 by Nicholas Brealey, an imprint of John Murray Press. An Hachette UK company.

Copyright © Nigel Cumberland 2019

The right of Nigel Cumberland to be identified as the Author of the Work has been asserted by him in accordance with the Copyright, Designs and Patents Act 1988.

British Library Cataloguing in Publication Data: a catalogue record for this title is available from the British Library.

Library of Congress Catalog Card Number: on file.

ISBN: 978 1 529 35323 5

eBook ISBN: 978 1 529 35325 9

US ebook ISBN: 978 1 529 35326 6

Every reasonable effort has been made to trace copyright holders, but if there are any errors or omissions, Nicholas Brealey will be pleased to insert the appropriate acknowledgement in any subsequent printings or editions.

Typeset by Cenveo® Publisher Services.

Printed and bound in the United States of America

John Murray Press policy is to use papers that are natural, renewable and recyclable products and made from wood grown in sustainable forests. The logging and manufacturing processes are expected to conform to the environmental regulations of the country of origin.

Nicholas Brealey Publishing
John Murray Press
Carmelite House
50 Victoria Embankment
London EC4Y 0DZ, UK
Tel: 020 3122 6000

Nicholas Brealey Publishing
Hachette Book Group
Market Place Center
53 State Street
Boston, MA 02109, USA
Tel: (617) 263 1834

www.nbuspublishing.com

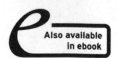

Also available
in ebook

This book is dedicated to my son, Zeb, to my stepdaughter, Yasmine, and to all those wishing to create a rich and meaningful life, filled with all the wealth you desire. May each of you find your unique path to financial and life success.

Little by little, a little becomes a lot.

– Tanzanian Proverb

Contents

About the author

Nigel Cumberland is the co-founder of The Silk Road Partnership, a leading global provider of executive coaching and leadership training solutions to some of the world's leading organizations. He has lived and worked in locations as diverse as Dubai, Hong Kong, Budapest, Santiago, Kuala Lumpur and Shanghai, gaining experiences and wisdom that have helped teach him what it takes to succeed in life.

Previously, Nigel worked as a multinational finance director with Coats plc, as well as for some of the world's leading recruitment firms, including Adecco. He holds the Master Practitioner status with the European Mentoring and Coaching Council and is a Fellow of the UK's Chartered Institute of Management Accountants. He co-created an award-winning recruitment firm based in Hong Kong and China, which he later sold to Hays plc. Educated at Cambridge University, UK, Nigel is an extensively qualified executive coach and leadership training professional.

He is the author of a large number of self-help and leadership books, among the most recent of which are: *The Ultimate Management Book* (John Murray Learning, 2018), *100 Things Successful People Do: Little Exercises for Successful Living* (John Murray Learning, 2016), *Secrets of Success at Work: 50 Techniques to Excel* (Hodder & Stoughton, 2014), *Finding and Hiring Talent in a Week* (John Murray Learning, 2016) and *Leading Teams in a Week* (John Murray Learning, 2016).

Nigel is married to a wonderful woman named Evelyn, who spends her time painting. He has two inspiring children – a son, Zeb, and a stepdaughter, Yasmine.

Introduction

'Earn before spending. Think before investing. Persist before quitting. Save before retiring. Give before dying.'

What does financial success mean to you? How important is being wealthy?

Whether or not you consider yourself financially successful depends on a mixture of your personal needs, goals and dreams, and the needs, goals and dreams of the important people in your life.

You've picked up this book because you want to create wealth, so let's break that down and think about what it means. Do you want to:

- buy a house and repay the loan as quickly as possible?
- build up enough investment income to retire from your day job?
- create a large enough nest egg to pay for the best education money can buy for your children?
- fund a lifestyle dream like becoming a musician or chef?
- build a property portfolio and live off the rental income?
- pay off your debts?
- own enough stocks, shares and financial investments to live off the dividends?
- buy a flashy sportscar?
- feel financially secure?
- create a foundation and give back to society?
- leave a large inheritance for your children?

I've coached hundreds of individuals and I've heard every financial dream you can imagine. I've listened to all the challenges and difficulties you face when you're trying to create wealth.

One thing is very clear. Too many people spend too long saving too little and consuming too much. Even people who, on paper at least, *should* be very wealthy are living in debt. You'll rarely meet anyone who will confidently announce: 'I have achieved my financial goals and created enough wealth.'

So this is your opportunity to sit down and think about your life goals, your unfulfilled dreams and wishes, and to ask yourself how you want to live and spend the rest of your time on this wonderful planet. This is your chance to map out your financial requirements, to explore who and what is driving you, and to delve into what you are willing to *do* in pursuit of your financial dreams.

This book is your guide. Through 100 short chapters, you will learn to make sense of the pieces you need to slot together to achieve *your* financial dreams. You will explore what wealth means to you through the following topics:

- Goals and dreams
- Mindset and behaviours
- Relationships and people
- Timeframes
- Types of wealth
- Investment practices
- Success and setbacks
- Working and retirement
- Helping and giving

How to use this book

Every chapter in this book features a new idea that will help you get closer to your goals. In each chapter, the ideas are introduced and explained on the first page and the second page features exercises and activities, some small and some large, for you to start doing today.

Don't overlook the activities. The tasks you've been set have been specifically designed to give you the optimal mindset, habits, skills, relationships and behaviours needed to maximize your chances of financial success. Some of them will surprise you, some will challenge you, others will seem simple and obvious. All of them are important in building the portfolio of skills you need for creating wealth. Completing them will set you on the path to developing a financially successful mindset and a wealth-focused 'to do' list. These things aren't easy to achieve and few people are willing to invest the required time and effort. Financially successful people do.

You'll find many activities to do straight away and some for later, depending on your financial situation and your financial goals. If an idea or suggestion doesn't seem helpful now, put it to one side and return to it later.

Who am I to talk about financial success?

This book draws on the wisdom I have gained from coaching and mentoring people from all over the world for over 20 years, people with all kinds of financial dreams and personal circumstances, from wealthy CEOs to struggling entrepreneurs, through full-time investors and recent graduates just starting out in their careers. All of them have something to share about the journey of creating wealth.

Their experiences combine with my own wisdom from 50 years on this planet and through some incredible financial highs and lows and the profound lessons I've learned through:

- investing in my own financial skills to become a Fellow of the UK's Chartered Institute of Management Accountants
- pushing myself to become a regional financial director with a FTSE100 company at the age of only 26
- investing large sums in a number of start-ups – some of which failed dramatically while others succeeded, such as selling a recruitment business in Asia to the UK's largest recruitment company, Hays plc, in 2006
- building a property development business on the side with my wife, investing in and renovating properties in various locations
- creating recurring income, including royalties, from my published books
- and most importantly, learning to have a meaningful relationship with wealth. It exists to help me live a fulfilling and meaningful life, and to enable me to help others achieve the same.

From all my work and experience, I have drawn up the most essential 100 things you need to do to achieve financial success and create an enriching and fulfilling life for yourself, those around you, and the world at large.

Good luck in your search for financial success and freedom. I hope all advice in this book helps you create the life you truly deserve.

100

THINGS

MILLIONAIRES DO

LITTLE LESSONS IN CREATING WEALTH

WHY DO YOU WANT TO BE WEALTHY?

'It's time to decide what you want from life.'

What motivated you to read this book? Do you want to be a millionaire, or do you just want to stop worrying about money?

It might not seem important but unless you really understand your motivation, you won't be able to set clear goals for your financial future.

Through my coaching I've heard every imaginable reason for building wealth:

- 'I don't want my children to live through the poverty I experienced when I was young.'
- 'I want to escape the daily struggles of living from pay cheque to pay cheque.'
- 'I want to be better off than my siblings.'
- 'I want to be more successful than my university friends.'
- 'I have a list of future needs and goals that require money to fund.'
- 'I want to be wealthy enough to be able to give it away to others.'
- 'I think wealth helps you feel valued and confident.'
- 'I have debts to pay off and I want to get on the property ladder.'

Your reasons will be personal to you. They might be covered in this list or they might be entirely different, there's no right and wrong. Every motivation is as valid as another. But whatever your reason for building wealth, no matter how seemingly trivial, selfish or insignificant, it is important to *know* it, so that you can be honest about what motivates and influences you.

The alternative is to risk wandering through life without knowing where to put your focus and attention.

> Making money for money's sake is meaningless. Know what building wealth means to you personally.

Put it into action

Map out your reasons for wanting to create wealth

Take a large piece of blank paper and create a mind map – an interconnected list of all the possible reasons why you want to be wealthier than you are today.

To help you complete this list, think about how you would answer the following questions:

- What unfulfilled dreams and desires do you have?
- What kind of life would you like to have in ten, twenty or thirty years' time?
- In what ways is your life today comfortable? And in what ways is it a financial struggle?
- Are you comparing yourself to others? Do you want to emulate somebody else?
- Are you trying to avoid something, for example financial distress that you have seen your parents or friends face?

Take your time to reflect, to create your list, and come back to it when new thoughts and insights come to you.

Which reasons do you want to act on?

When your list is done it's time to review it and identify the reasons that are most important to you. Be honest when you do this. You are identifying core values here and you have to be comfortable with what you allow to drive you.

If you find it hard to focus in on what is most important, try coming at it from a different perspective. Do any of your reasons make you uncomfortable? Can you eliminate anything that feels negative or unhealthy where the reason is driven by ego rather than what really matters to you?

Talk with your loved ones and friends

Sense-check your own thinking by listening to others, or do the exercise with other people. Their reasons will almost certainly surprise you and give you food for thought.

WHAT DOES WEALTH MEAN TO YOU?

'Wealth enables you to live the life you always longed for.'

When you think about being wealthy, what kinds of thoughts and feelings come to mind? Do you imagine some kind of blissful state where everyday stresses miraculously vanish and you're free to live your dreams?

In my experience, that's often the spin people place on being wealthy, until they really think about it. Often there are surprising worries bubbling just below the surface.

Take a look at these lists – again drawn from real-life coaching conversations.

Typical first impression of being wealthy	Typical deeper reaction
'I'll be able to live the life of my dreams.'	'I'm scared of what I'd actually do.'
'I'll have the freedom to be me.'	'I will lose myself.'
'I'll be able to show off.'	'Other people will be jealous.'
'I'll be able to do anything I want.'	'I will be overwhelmed.'
'Everybody will be my friend.'	'Other people will want my money.'
'Anything will be possible.'	'I'd have no idea where to start.'
'I'll have no more money-related panic attacks.'	'I don't trust myself to look after it.'
'I'll be happy at last.'	'I don't deserve it.'

Nearly everyone can come up with wonderful and meaningful reasons for wanting to be wealthy, but when you actually visualize it, the first impression can quickly turn to mixed feelings.

It's perfectly natural for something so life-changing to provoke a mixture of feelings from hope and joy to concern and fear. What's important is for you to work through your own range of responses to ensure that there's nothing in the background holding you back.

> It is OK if you are unclear about what becoming wealthy makes you think and feel.

Put it into action

Be honest with yourself

Carry out a word association exercise, ideally on a large piece of blank paper. Write down each of the following phrases, one at a time.

Making money

Becoming wealthier

Managing and looking after my wealth

Being rich

In what ways do they produce positive and exciting thoughts and feelings within you? Or do they raise concerns, worries and negative thoughts and feelings? Write down all the associated words and phrases on the paper.

Reflect on what you've written. Don't be surprised or embarrassed by any of your thoughts and feelings. It's human to be both excited and positive, and at the same time worried and concerned. You are likely to hold a mix of both wonderful feelings and anxieties.

The positive ideas you list can energize and motivate you, so keep them close and return to them regularly on this journey to help you stay focused on your goal.

You should explore any concerns, fears and worries you identify. Work through them as you go through this book.

HOW WEALTHY DO YOU WANT TO BE?

'The world is filled to the brim with wealth. You just have to go out and get your share.'

When will you be rich enough, that's the million dollar question. Or the 2.4 million dollar question, to be more accurate. In 2017, financial services firm Charles Schwab interviewed 1,000 Americans aged 21 to 75 and discovered that on average, the respondents wanted $1.4 million to feel financially comfortable and $2.4 million to consider themselves wealthy.

In another 2017 survey by the salary benchmarking website emolument.com, the average twenty-something British worker said they would feel wealthy if they were earning £93,000 per year. For older workers this figure rose to £370,000 per year.

These numbers vary by country, reflecting differing costs of living. The same survey revealed that workers in India consider themselves rich when earning the equivalent of £25,000 per year.

You may have already guessed it. There is no single answer to what being wealthy means. The important thing is what wealth means to you, and where you decide to set your financial target.

Knowing how much money will satisfy you is a very personal decision.

Put it into action

Set yourself a target

I have always loved the idea in *Alice in Wonderland* that if you don't know where you're going, any road will take you there. By working hard, saving and investing your income, you will most probably become wealthier than you are today. But where will you end up? Will you be financially comfortable enough to be able to retire, travel the world, donate to your favourite charities and help your children?

To be sure of living the life you dream of, it is essential to have at least an approximate calculation of how much wealth you need to create. Do this by reflecting on what you want to fund, purchase and hold in reserve.

- What are the key things you need to pay for? Examples might include a house, university educations for your kids, a fund for medical bills or enough to travel every year.
- Do you want to achieve a certain level of annual income – income that is from investments and assets, not from working in a job?
- Do you have an overall financial target, like the respondents in the Charles Schwab survey?

Don't worry if you can't calculate a precise figure. I struggle with this too. Instead I've set myself a target of simply ensuring my wealth increases every year and to feel that I can live off my wealth without having to sell any of my investments.

Speak with a financial adviser

It can be a good idea to explore this with your certified public accountant (CPA) or independent financial advisor (IFA). Using Excel spreadsheets or online software, a professional can help you map out your financial requirements and estimate how much wealth you need to build up over a specified timeframe.

YOU DESERVE THIS

'Ask the universe what you need. If you really believe it's yours, it will be delivered.'

No matter whether you believe you'll be successful or believe you'll fail, you'll always be right. Self-belief is key to how your life plays out. Quite simply, you achieve what you *believe* you will achieve.

Too many people struggle with life and money, unable to find a way out of their situation. They stop believing that any other outcome is possible. And to make matters worse, we all tend to be our own harshest critic. It makes me want to cry when I hear stories about:

- the talented musician who doesn't believe he can make it in the music industry and struggles to make ends meet in mundane jobs
- the senior banker who self-sabotages his career, thinking he's not worthy of a senior position.

There's a saying that the only place your dreams become impossible is in your own head. To become wealthy, you must believe that you *deserve* to be wealthy.

Learn and practise what it takes to build self-belief and you will lay solid foundations for building wealth.

> The world is full of 'almost successful' and 'could have been successful' people, held back by self-doubt.

Put it into action

Be honest with yourself

It's not enough just to want to be wealthy and have a financial target in mind. You will have discovered by now that your feelings about wealth can include self-doubt, disbelief and even fear. These negative feelings need to be addressed, as left unchecked they can grow and de-rail you.

Talking to other people can help you deal with your internal voice. Open up and talk about your doubts with someone you trust. Allow yourself to understand and sense-check your thinking patterns. By talking to someone, you will probably find that your anxieties are completely normal. After all, you are leaving your comfort zone and embarking on a mission to build wealth. It's only natural to experience fears and concerns.

Seek help and support

If you're finding it hard to overcome your doubts and suffer from a lack of self-belief, find a coach or therapist who can provide cognitive behavioural therapy (CBT). I have used CBT in my work for many years and it is very effective at changing the patterns of behaviour and thinking that cause negative feelings and beliefs. As these patterns change, this in turn changes the way you feel.

This type of therapy can be completed in a short timeframe, through a series of one-on-one conversations.

HAVE CLEAR GOALS AND A PLAN

'Every noteworthy accomplishment starts life as a simple goal – a goal that turns into a specific plan of action.'

Wealth creation doesn't happen by chance, planning is key. In a 2018 survey by the asset management firm Legg Mason, 77% of investors said they save and invest with specific goals in mind. If you're not the type of person who religiously writes to-do lists, you need to become like that.

Going with the flow and seeing what happens is not an option. You'll end up spending all of your energy on tasks, and with people, that aren't bringing you closer to your goals. Details and plans are going to become your new friends.

Planning is a decision. A conscious choice to be structured in how you use your time, energy and other resources. It's a process of leaving no stone unturned, of ensuring you have thought of all the details. There's always room for good fortune and unexpected luck, but these tend to happen more when you're structured and adopt a planning mindset.

Financial success *can* come in a random unplanned way. You might win the lottery, but even a lottery winner needs a plan to stop their wealth disappearing through their fingers.

Put it into action

Planning starts with detailed goals

Think again about your financial goals. They might just be fluffy-sounding dreams such as 'I want a million dollars in savings', 'I want to retire early' or 'I want to own a range of properties'. That's OK, these are just first drafts.

Turn these into more detailed and specific goals using the SMART goals framework. For each goal ask yourself whether it's:

* Specific and clear enough
* Measurable, so that you know when it's achieved
* Attainable, and, if not, how can you make it attainable
* Realistic and relevant to your circumstances and life
* Timeframe bound with a clearly stated 'achieve by' date.

Write down your answers. You can now re-write your goals as detailed plans. The vague goal of 'owning a range of properties' might become SMART like this:

My property goal

* To create a $1 million property portfolio ...
* over the next five years ...
* through buying a number of small buy-to-let properties ...
* in university towns ...
* taking bank mortgage financing ...
* and with the deposits coming from my savings.

Wear a project management hat

You can create more detailed plans for every SMART goal, breaking down tasks into quarterly or monthly targets. You might benefit from creating a Gantt chart to capture the tasks and activities you need to carry out, typically by week or month.

IF IT'S TOO GOOD TO BE TRUE ...

'Be careful about taking short cuts. They could lead you up blind alleys.'

When it comes to money, if it sounds too good to be true, it probably is. There is no magic potion or short cut to creating wealth.

With almost every aspect of our lives on demand these days, we've become impatient, and impatience has made us more susceptible to 'invest and double your money' messages. Scams like these are far too common:

- Ponzi or pyramid schemes where you're promised lovely annual returns or profits of maybe 10% or 20% per annum. Little do you realize that the only thing funding these returns is new investors' money. There is no real investing going on.
- 'Help me with my inheritance' pleas where you receive an email or phone call from someone seeking your help. They've inherited millions and just need some money from you to pay the fees.
- Any other kind of 'amazing' opportunities, such as investing in a gold mine or some tech start-up's new invention.

No matter how convincing they sound – and actually, they do sometimes sound convincing – beware of anything offering you a risk-free investment, guaranteed returns, easy money or a 'cannot fail' boast. It can fail, and it probably will.

> If it sounds too good to be true, it probably is.

Put it into action

Avoid acting out of desperation or greed

No matter how desperately you want to change your financial fortunes, never jump into dodgy or questionable investments. Greed can easily overwhelm your senses and turn your head with the promise of a quick win or large guaranteed return. Learn to pause and reflect. However much pressure you're under to invest NOW, just sleep on it.

If in doubt, seek advice

Try to only work through banks or other reputable financial advisors. Never entertain strangers who cold-call or send you a spam email. If they claim to be calling from your bank, put the phone down and call your bank to verify.

Every country's financial conduct authority is concerned about scams and they usually have a webpage offering advice and a helpline to help those who fear they may be or have been scammed. Call them before transferring any money.

Apart from the risk of being cheated out of your money, investing in dodgy schemes could leave you accused of knowingly breaking the law by acting unethically. We'll learn more about this later in the book.

WEALTH DOES NOT ENSURE HAPPINESS

'True wealth is a life of riches made up of fulfilling moments, experiences and relationships.'

Extra money *does* equate to more happiness, at least when you start from a low base. This has been confirmed by researchers from Purdue University who carried out an enormous survey of 1.7 million people across 64 countries, with the results reported in the peer-reviewed international journal of science *Nature*. They concluded that people are happiest when they earn about US$75,000–95,000 per year.

But once you become richer, don't be surprised if increases in your bank balance no longer make you feel better. The study in *Nature*, which correlates with other studies, found that people's satisfaction with life and well-being declined as their incomes exceeded US$95,000 per year.

That's a bit surprising, isn't it, given that we're constantly made to feel that the rich have more amazing lives than we do.

There are at least three reasons why more wealth does not correlate with increased happiness:

- More money = more stress. The more you have, the more you have to look after, remember and protect. And as you become richer, other people may treat you differently, wanting more from you.
- More money leads to constant comparisons with others which lead to feelings of envy and jealousy. Sometimes it's better just not to get on the treadmill in the first place.
- More money means you quickly grow bored of the things you acquire. Being able to buy a brand-new sports car or take holidays at your own ski chalet will make you happy but all evidence suggests that happiness declines as soon as you get used to material things or experiences. Economists call it the 'hedonic treadmill'.

It is OK if you are having trouble believing that money is not the source of happiness.

Put it into action

Identify what brings you happiness in the first place

Before having or spending your wealth, identify those aspects of your life that make you happy and fulfilled. It might be:

- Being with certain people such as family, friends, neighbours or colleagues
- Helping people in need
- Having fulfilling paid work
- Having free time full of activities, hobbies and pastimes
- Spending time in particular locations and environments.

Focus your wealth on the sources of your happiness

The secret to being rich *and* happy is ensuring that as you grow your wealth, you invest in those activities that bring you fulfilment and joy. Investing in rewarding family time, the education of your children, charity work, a meaningful career or wonderful travels aligns your financial growth with a deeper purpose.

Be worried if 'showing off your wealth' makes you happy

If being more financially successful than others gives you a 'high' and leads you to vainly buy things and experiences simply to show off, it sounds as if your ego is driving your actions and behaviours. There's no benefit and nothing meaningful to gain from finding happiness and fulfilment in simply being wealthy and/or wealthier than others. Don't end up like Ebenezer Scrooge in Dickens' *A Christmas Carol*.

WHAT ARE YOU WAITING FOR?

'The only way to drive a car is to turn on the ignition and take off the handbrake.'

Getting wealthy takes time and the longer you delay, the harder it becomes. If you keep passing on investment opportunities, or your typical response to financial planning is to put it off till later, you're not alone. Spending money is fun, planning NOT to spend it isn't half such a thrill – on the surface at least.

This is a big mistake – not getting into the game early is probably the single biggest thing holding people back from achieving financial success.

There are lots of good reasons for putting it off of course:

- Money's tight and just getting by day to day is the priority.
- You don't fully understand the opportunity.
- You don't have time to make long-term plans.
- You're too young to worry about the future.
- You're afraid of the unknown.

With money, sometimes not doing anything is the right thing, but other times, being slow to act means you miss opportunities. The bottom line is, the earlier you start making your money work for you, whether it's saving, trading stocks and shares, or buying property, the sooner you'll hit your wealth target.

The earlier you start building your wealth, the closer you will be to achieving your goal.

Put it into action

Figure out what's holding you back

What's been holding you back from fully committing to building wealth? Reflect on how you make financial decisions. Is there a pattern behind your inaction?

- Do you find it hard to get out of the NOW and think about the future?
- Are you worried about leaving your comfort zone and entering the unknown?
- Are you averse to risk?

If not now, when?

There are often very good reasons for delaying – after all, making money involves risks. This book's advice will help you make wise financial choices, balancing risk versus opportunities, so that you can get the timing right.

If it's more like reluctance on your part, or you're just too confused, overworked or scared to act, you may benefit from spending time with a coach.

Do something today

If you are delaying making a financial plan, or even making a big commitment like buying your first investment property, write a list of information you need and the tasks you have to do. Breaking down your goals into smaller and easier to implement tasks is a brilliant way to get started.

TRACK SPENDING AGAINST A FORECAST

'A budget helps show you where your money is coming from and where it's going.'

It can be hard to keep track of spending. With some payments on your credit card and others by direct debit, you may never actually see a single list of all your outgoings.

Maybe it helps to know that if you don't monitor and plan your household spending, you're not alone. A 2013 Gallup survey found that only 32% of Americans maintain some kind of household budget. That's a lot of people who have no idea whether they're going to have enough left over at the end of each month to pay the bills, let alone create a surplus.

If you're not on top of it, you risk overspending. According to the UK's Office for National Statistics, UK households in 2017, for the first time in 30 years, spent more than they received in income. The average difference was £900. I bet most families had no idea.

Ignoring how much you spend each month is just putting off potential bad news, and worse – keeping yourself in the dark about your financial situation means you'll never be in a position to start building wealth.

Creating a spending plan and forecast is time well spent.

Put it into action

Keep track of your actual cashflow

Even though you're reading this book, you may not think of yourself as a numbers person. That's about to change. This is where you lay the foundations for your future wealth. You're going to start keeping a running summary of your money flows.

There are no rules to this so just do it any way you feel comfortable:

- On paper, the old-school way.
- On an Excel spreadsheet. If you're not a fan of creating Excel tables with different formulas, there are some free online templates available.
- Through an online budgeting app. Your bank might have one you can use or you can find examples on www.thisismoney.co.uk in the UK, and www.mint.com in the US. A good app is like an Excel spreadsheet – you enter all your expenses and create monthly and annual totals.
- Some banks, such as Monzo (UK) or GoBank (US), automatically create summaries of your debit and credit card expenses by area, e.g. food, travel and clothes. The danger with this is that you forget to include cash expenses or expenditures made using other cards.

Create a forecast of what you want to spend and earn

Budgeting tools can also include forecasts so you can estimate your future income flows and outgoings. Your income might include monthly salary, annual bonus, dividend payments and any other income you plan to earn. Your forecast expenses are what you plan to spend on each particular expense such as food, clothes, holidays, utility bills, car expenses, etc.

For a comprehensive budget you should estimate all your outgoings, including any money you invest in savings schemes. You could do this at the start of the year or at the start of each quarter. You'll then be able to compare your actual outflows and inflows against your forecast and start to understand the reasons for any gaps or differences.

Lay the foundations of your wealth and take control of your finances.

MOST MILLIONAIRES START FROM NOTHING

'An empty wallet never stops successful people. A lack of ambition and an empty mindset stops many others.'

According to a global survey by Fidelity Investments, one of the world's largest financial services groups, 86% of millionaires made their own wealth. In other words, nearly nine out of ten wealthy people did not inherit their money, they started with nothing, and in many cases came from extreme poverty.

JK Rowling was penniless when she penned her *Harry Potter* stories. In her 2008 Harvard University commencement speech, she spoke about the depths of her situation, being out of work, penniless, and realizing that the only thing stopping her being destitute was that she still had a roof over her head.

Rags-to-riches stories are more common than you'd imagine. The next time you feel down about not having any savings or having a low salary, take heart. Many millionaires were in equally challenging situations before they found financial freedom.

So if you don't need money to create wealth, what do you need? That depends on who you are and how you want to create your wealth. It all comes down to mindset, skills, education, passion, purpose, habits, thinking and ideas. You'll find lots of inspiration throughout this book.

Anyone, whatever their current financial situation, can become wealthy.

Put it into action

Enough of the 'poor me'

Psychologists, such as the late Dr Nolen-Hoeksema, a professor at Yale University, refer to 'poor me' feelings as rumination, the tendency to dwell on the sources of your problems – what you *don't* have rather than possible solutions.

Prolonged periods of rumination and feeling bad about your circumstances are not healthy. Dr Nolen-Hoeksema's research linked it to all kinds of mood and behaviourial issues including eating disorders, substance abuse and depression.

It's important to stop focusing on what you don't have and instead focus your mind on what you need to do. Busy yourself with what you want to become, create and acquire. Be like Dwayne 'The Rock' Johnson who once said: '1995. $7 bucks in my pocket. I knew two things: I'm broke as hell and one day I won't be.'

Take an inventory of what you have

Letting go of the 'poor me' mindset might take nothing more than reading this book, or it might take time and even therapy to work through the underlying reasons.

You could start by writing down a list of what you have going for you. Think of all the positive attributes and skills you possess. Make it as varied as your dreams, goals, education, work experience, technical skills, creativity, network of contacts and family connections.

Don't dwell on the problems – focus on the solutions.

DETERMINATION IS YOUR FINANCIAL SUPERPOWER

'Nothing can hold you back when your willpower's alive and kicking.'

Determination and willpower are your greatest allies in the quest to build wealth. They boil down to one thing – the ability to do something that other people would struggle to complete.

Willpower is a muscle and it's as important and large as any in your body. It needs using, developing and strengthening through regular, repetitive and conscious use so that it becomes a habit. Imagine how formidable and focused you would be if your determination was as habitual as brushing your teeth.

Becoming wealthy can be stressful and studies show that when you're stressed you fall back on your habits, no matter whether they're good or bad for you. So it's essential to your success that you've got the right habits in place.

Exercise your willpower regularly. Push yourself to your limits to build determination. Your bank balance will thank you.

Put it into action

Practise until it becomes automatic

Turning anything into a habit takes time and effort. Much of my leadership training revolves around helping people adopt and develop new habits. Willpower is one of the harder habits to master but you can make it easier.

- Be clear on what aspect of your willpower you're trying to strengthen. Pin it down to specifics, like having the discipline to save before you spend or not give up so easily on tasks at work. Write down exactly what it is you want to achieve and then push yourself to do it.
- Monitor yourself and celebrate successes. This can be a private thing, or you could use an accountability partner, someone you trust who will hold you accountable and who you report to each week or month to share examples of how well, or not, you're doing.

Focus on your daily work and successes

If you only focus on your future goals and needs, your determination may weaken. This happens when you fail to recognize how well you're overcoming your *daily* challenges and struggles. Being conscious of your everyday successes keeps your determination growing, as it's a constant reminder that you can persist and succeed.

When coaching leaders I encourage them to have both longer-term goals and daily, weekly and monthly targets. At the end of each week, it helps to write down recent examples of the roadblocks, challenges and barriers you've faced. Listing examples of where you've shown determination and willpower, no matter how small and trivial, will help you grow.

Recognize and celebrate your successes.

FRIENDS CAN MAKE OR BREAK YOU

'Some people energize you and drive you forward. Others poison and drown your ambitions.
Choose wisely.'

There's a theory that each of us is the average of the five people we spend most time with. Can you imagine if you hung out with some of the world's most respected billionaires, like Bill Gates, Richard Branson and Jack Ma?

Science backs up the idea that the people we socialize with have an incredible impact upon us. A 2013 study in the journal *Psychological Science* concluded that having strong-willed friends could increase your self-control, as if just being in their presence strengthens your willpower. It works because they're serving as your subconscious role models.

Psychologists call it social influence and it refers to the ways you adjust your actions and ideas to conform to the expectations of a particular social group. Do you:

- buy clothes or foods to be like your colleagues?
- keep quiet about your ambitions in case your family belittle you for dreaming of being rich?
- spend your weekends doing activities that you don't totally enjoy simply to play along with your friends?

It's a good idea to reflect on your relationships and consider which serve you in a positive way. Explore which of your friends and acquaintances have values, mindsets and behaviours that are aligned with your own. Social influence can be harnessed to support you on your journey to creating wealth.

Don't allow other people's insecurities, small-mindedness or lack of belief to hold you back from fulfilling your own needs and following your own path.

Put it into action

Pull away from toxic people

Don't spend time with people who make fun of your goals or how you choose to spend your time, energy and money in pursuit of a better life.

If you know that spending time with toxic people, jealous friends, bitter colleagues and insecure siblings is not helping you, then break the pattern. Be nice, be diplomatic, but give them space. You may feel obligated or guilty pulling away but if you have to choose, is it creating the life you want or not rocking the boat?

Surround yourself with people who support and believe in you

Allow yourself to meet and be drawn to like-minded souls who appreciate your ambitions, desire for a better life and more financial freedom.

To be clear, I am not suggesting that you walk away from your old life and give up all your friends in order to make new ones. It's a balance. Perhaps you could gradually increase the time and support you get from those friends – old and new – who get you, and appreciate what you're trying to achieve.

STOP LEAKING MONEY

'Look for and seal up all those little holes that are causing your tyres to deflate.'

Imagine if your bank account leaked money. Nothing drastic, just a few dollars or pounds every day. It wouldn't cause a panic, but it would amount to quite a lot of money over time.

And I bet it's already happening. We all leak money, trust me. No one is totally immune to spending cash on things that don't matter or don't get used.

Often they're only small amounts, but when you're creating wealth, you need every dollar. Writing off the little bits spent here and there is a big mistake.

So next time you're walking past your favourite coffee shop, ask yourself how much your latte habit is costing you. It's spare change every day but adds up to hundreds over the course of 12 months. And that's money that could be working for you to help you achieve your financial goals.

Same with your gym membership for that club where you train two or three times a month, or your unread magazine subscription.

Don't let the little leaks drain your wealth away.

Put it into action

Trim the fat

Let's do a review of your spending. Start by double-checking your direct debits and autopay instructions. If there are any surprises in there, cancel them.

Monitor yourself daily so you know what you're paying for or signing up to. Pause on any purchases you don't think you really need.

You could try using an app such as usebean.com to help you track old subscriptions you no longer want to continue.

Take an inventory

Most people don't even know half the stuff they have so why not do an inventory of what you own? I guarantee you will find things you could sell or give away, or that you already own things that will save you a purchase. There are lots of little discoveries you could make that will make, or save, money.

Curb your impulses

Tempting as it is to make impulse purchases, it often doesn't work out. It's easy to be caught up in the moment or feel under pressure because a sale price is ending. Purchases made in the heat of the moment often result in buyer's remorse. Who hasn't signed up for faster broadband only to discover your internet speed's barely changed?

Remember those current accounts like Monzo that allow you to monitor your spending in creative ways? Try switching to one of those, or check out an app like Revolut. Now's the time to curb your buying habits.

SAVE BEFORE SPENDING

'Only spend money you've already earned.'

How much money do you save each month? Sadly, none of us saves enough, and far too many people have no savings at all.

In the US, a 2018 survey by bankrate.com revealed that 25% of 18- to 53-year-olds have no savings, nothing set by. Nothing to fall back on. Another 25% only have enough savings to cover three months of living expenses.

There's a similar picture in the UK, where 2018 research by Skipton Building Society found that one in four adults have no savings, and one in ten spend more than they earn. A 2017 survey by the Financial Conduct Authority found that one in three in the UK have savings of less than £2,000.

Saving is the cornerstone of becoming wealthy. If you can't save, it won't happen for you. Sadly, for many, especially the young, it's not getting any easier; salaries are flat, housing and living costs are on the rise, and temptations to spend money are all around us. But here's the good news. You don't have to set aside much each month to make a difference, just the act of saving will start to get you into the wealth mindset, and with the gift of time, those small sums you put aside early on have even longer to grow into something significant.

> Saving is the cornerstone of becoming wealthy.

Put it into action

Develop a 'savings mindset'

It's tempting to question the value of saving, especially when it means giving yourself financial hardship now in order to save just a small amount. Once you've reached the end of this book and fine-tuned your financial thinking, you'll want to save. When you understand the how, what and why of growing your wealth, you'll get why this is essential. And as you create your own financial goals, you'll have clear reasons to save.

Put money aside when you're paid

Better to start small than not at all. Start now and make it a fixed habit rather than something left to chance at the end of each month. Never wait until the end of the month to see how much is left after your outgoings have been paid. Do the opposite; set aside at least 10% of your monthly salary as soon as you're paid. Set up an auto-transfer of 10% into a separate savings account timed to happen the day after pay day. You won't be alone. According to Skipton Building Society, 25% of Brits do this, using direct debit to automatically transfer some of their salary.

How much should you save? Start with 10% of your salary, but in truth, start with as much as possible! Only you know what your essential expenses and financial commitments are. If you're on a very low salary, you might think 10% is too much. Make it 5% then. Alternatively, if you're being well paid, you could (and should) save a higher percentage.

Save salary increases and bonuses

If you're lucky enough to be paid bonuses at different points in the year, consider putting all or most straight into your savings account. Maybe even put some into a pension scheme, or in the US, increase your 401(k) contributions.

BE READY FOR A LONELY JOURNEY

'The road to success can be very lonely. Be ready for days of hard work, of being misunderstood
and struggling to make time for others.'

Achieving any kind of success is hard. It takes long hours of work, missed social events, being misunderstood and feeling alone. If you've not experienced any of these yet, just give it time.

You may not be physically alone, but those around you may struggle to understand and appreciate your financial goals, and misunderstand what you need to do to achieve them. They might just see you being more careful with money or hanging out less than before.

You may even lose people along the way, either because they don't get it, or because you choose to pull away because they've become jealous, negative or unsupportive.

One thing's for sure, you'll meet many setbacks on the way. There will inevitably be a moment when the markets seem like they're about to crash on your investments. You'll feel alone then. At times like that, you may even wish you *were* alone!

> Creating wealth takes time, energy and focus.

15

Put it into action

Accept what you don't want to change

It's entirely your decision to go down this potentially lonely path. It's a trade-off and only you can find your balance. A theme running through this book is that creating wealth takes time, energy and focus. That's time and energy that would otherwise be available for other people in your life. It is your decision what you choose to focus on.

Don't lose those you love and care about

We've already seen that money doesn't necessarily bring happiness, so bear that in mind and don't allow your drive for financial success to destroy relationships in your life.

Seek to understand, then be understood

Reach out to people and try to understand how they're feeling. They may sense that you're neglecting them or feel that you're moving away from them as you chase your financial dreams.

Give them time to understand that you're still you, that you still care for them, but that your priorities have changed. You have less free time and (ironically) less money than before.

You need not be totally alone

Just as Warren Buffett had Charlie Munger, Steve Wozniak had Steve Jobs, and Larry Page had Sergey Brin, perhaps you could build up your wealth in partnership with someone else. For some people this works well, for others it might cause a clash.

MASTER THE ART OF SELLING

'We spend our entire lives selling to others; we sell our ideas, opinions, views – things of value.'

Financially successful people are great salespeople. They typically have very highly sharpened persuasion and influencing skills that are essential in helping them win over other people and overcome challenges on the path to financial success.

Honing your sales skills will help you in a variety of situations:

- Demonstrating to your boss that you're worthy of a promotion
- Pushing your boss to pay you the salary your work deserves
- Presenting your business ideas so that others support them
- Inspiring people to work with you to help you achieve your dreams
- Winning new customers for your start-up business
- Persuading a private bank or broker to take you on as a client
- Attracting investors and shareholders to invest in your start-up
- Convincing yourself to do what is needed to achieve your goals.

Not everyone can present like Steve Jobs. Fortunately, you don't have to be a super confident extrovert to have great sales skills. Quiet introverts can be just as effective in sales situations, particularly at building rapport and relationships. Many of today's well-known billionaires, such as Bill Gates, Mark Zuckerberg and Jack Ma, aren't natural extroverts. Part of their success has been in allowing their work to sell itself, to speak up when needed, and to seek the help of others in convincing and persuading people.

The important thing is to accept that you are unique and to try to understand yourself.

16

Put it into action

Work on your communication skills

Selling is all about communication and it never hurts to improve your ability to communicate well. One of the most important communication skills you can work on is practising your active listening. This is the art of deliberately and consciously showing the person you're with that you hear what they are saying and feeling.

Be authentic

Bank managers, investors and future employees don't expect you to be an amazing salesperson but they do expect you to be authentic and real. We are all naturally drawn to, and want to work with, people who listen and care and have passion for what they believe in.

Put yourself in other people's shoes

When you need to win someone over, don't go into full on sales mode. Look at things from their perspective. What help do they need? What problems and challenges are they facing? How could you create value for them?

Before asking a bank for a loan for example, start by asking yourself: 'Why will they buy my request? What will cause them to trust me? How can I help them with their problems, goals and challenges?'

Gain some hands-on sales experience

If you're starting out in your career and you're not sure what path to choose, consider taking a sales role. It's a great opportunity to learn how to handle the challenges involved in winning over, influencing and persuading other people. Plus you'll have plenty of opportunity to experience rejection and build the resilience you need to keep going against all odds.

FORM YOUR OWN VIEW OF DEBT

'It's amazing how some people treat debt like the enemy, while others fall deeply in love with their credit cards and payday loans.'

Some people seem quite chilled about taking on debt. When I was young, I only saw people borrowing and delaying payments when they were truly desperate. It was rare for anyone to seek a loan to pay for non-essentials. Not any longer. Today being in debt is an acceptable lifestyle choice, constantly promoted in the media with numerous adverts urging us to:

* Buy now and pay later
* Take out a 12-month interest free loan
* Start using a new credit card in return for free gifts
* Borrow at Christmas time to pay for the turkey and presents
* Get a payday loan to tide you over for a few days.

This all adds up. According to a 2017 www.comparethemarket.com survey, the average UK household owes £8,000 in consumer debt, made up of credit card bills, car loans, payday loans but excluding house mortgage loans. In the US, the figures are similar, with average credit card debt alone equalling US$4,293 per American in a 2018 survey by experian.com.

What's your view on debt? Does it make you uncomfortable? There isn't a right or wrong answer but it's important to understand how you feel about it.

Debt has a role to play in wealth creation, as you will see.

Put it into action

Understand debt

Later on I'll share advice about how to manage and reduce your debts, and help you ensure that any debt you take on is a wise decision. But first you need to understand debt so you can appreciate the different types and the costs of any money you are offered.

So what is debt? At its most simple, debt is an amount of money borrowed by you from various possible sources or lenders. It might be secured or unsecured debt.

- Secured debt is borrowings linked to your assets such as your house or car. The asset is a guarantee or collateral. Fail to repay your loan and the lender can take the asset.
- Unsecured debt is not linked to anything you own, for example borrowing on your credit card. Typically this involves paying higher rates of interest because the lender takes on the risk of you not repaying without an asset they can seize in return.

You need to understand as many details of any debt as possible, including the array of interest rates, fees, penalties, timeframes and rules that come with the different types of borrowing, from high interest payday loans and credit cards through to fixed interest mortgages. Make time to research before taking on new debt and talk to someone such as a CPA or IFA.

Come to an informed view

Once you have better knowledge about debt, spend some time reviewing your borrowings. Explore your past choices and look at when and how you took on debt. Build up your 'debt wisdom' and become an expert in what it means to take on and be in debt.

You will never again be taken in by those warm and appealing adverts encouraging you to borrow a little more for that holiday in the sun.

BE A REMARKABLE EMPLOYEE

'If you want to be highly valued at work, create more value than you are being paid to produce.'

If you want to be a millionaire, don't give up the day job. It may not be the best paid in the world, but it's where you are today and it's where you may be for some time to come.

Your day job is your training ground for building wealth. Go to work every day with a success mindset. Become indispensable. Aim to be perceived as the star performer who deservedly receives the maximum levels of salary increases, bonuses, job promotions and any other forms of recognition. While you're there, develop the habits of impressing and inspiring those around you and always surpassing goals and expectations. These are habits you will need in the future.

You may not become a millionaire through this job, but you should aim to be well rewarded and recognized as you build your skills through it.

What's the alternative? You switch off and coast because you know you'll be moving on. Taking it easy has its benefits: less stress, more spare time, energy to pursue other interests. But you risk becoming lazy and that's the opposite of the millionaire mindset.

If you're going to do anything in life, give it everything. Go the extra mile.

18

Put it into action

Go the extra mile

Even some of the top leaders I coach need reminding to go the extra mile. Here's a quick checklist of things you can do:

- Be physically present. Don't arrive late in the morning or disappear for long lunches. Be wary of slacking off to use your time on other business initiatives.
- Be mentally present. Avoid spending time at your desk focused on your own money-making activities like trading or buying property.
- Give more than 100%. It is not enough to simply be fully present. Give all of your time and energy, up to and including your last day in the job. Don't accept that it's OK to cut corners.
- Add value with your personality. Be the colleague people are drawn towards – someone who's interesting and interested, speaks up productively in discussions and wants to help.
- Go home on time. Yes, you can still leave the office on time. No one's saying you have to work until midnight every day.

Once you have left the office you're free to focus on your own ventures and money-making ideas like creating a side hustle, investing in assets or learning new skills.

Negotiate your salary

When you go the extra mile, you can have the courage to ask for the salary you feel you deserve. There's advice later on about how to sell this to your boss.

BE CAREFUL WITH CASH

'No self-made millionaire has ever made their wealth from a savings account.'

Cash might be king, but not necessarily a wealthy king. Twenty years ago, you could leave money in the bank and watch it grow at a rate of at least 5% a year thanks to high rates of interest on deposits. You could simply sit back and feel like you were getting richer – although in reality, with high price inflation at the time, your bank balance might have been increasing but not your spending power.

Today it's different. Interest rates on deposits are very low and sometimes close to zero. Money in the bank is like left luggage: when you come back, it's exactly how you left it. Current levels of price inflation might be low, but that provides little compensation when earning negligible interest.

Even with its low return, holding cash can seem relatively safe compared with the risk of an investment that doesn't pay off – and it is safe – but the inherent problem with cash is that it will never get you rich. It will help you spin on the spot but not propel you forward. Risk = reward and the higher the risk, the higher the potential reward.

The important thing is to be ready for when things don't go to plan, and to have a structured approach to risk so that one setback doesn't sink you.

19

Put it into action

How much cash should you hold?

How much cash you hold is a very personal decision. I can't answer it for you, but after many years of experience, here is what I've learned:

- If you have a better and more productive use for your cash, use it. If not, keep it in your savings account ready to be used later.
- If you're looking to increase your total wealth, holding cash is a poor choice. If not, leaving it in the bank might be an ideal option.
- If you're very risk averse you might find it too stressful to tie up all your funds in investments that hold some risk. Holding some in cash might be a necessary option.
- The 'rainy day' analogy has some truth to it. Overused as it is, you might need to hold cash as an emergency reserve.
- It is often wiser to use your cash than take out a debt. Why take out a loan if you have the available cash to buy a new car?

All this discussion of what to do with your cash might seem like a lucky problem to have, when you have no money. The advice in this book will help you increase your wealth and eventually you will have some excess cash that isn't tied up in daily living expenses. Roll on!

ROLL UP YOUR SLEEVES

'Financial success is often avoided because it is dressed in overalls and smells like hard work.'

Working four hours a week sounds great, but the experiences of numerous millionaires and billionaires is that success takes effort and time. Mark Cuban is reputed not to have taken a vacation for seven years, and to have worked through the night learning to code. Elon Musk has spoken about having to work 80 to 100 hours every week.

Studies confirm that the wealthy have a strong work ethic. Princeton's Professor of Sociology, Dalton Conley, found that those with higher incomes work more hours than those on lower incomes and research by Nobel Prize-winning Daniel Kahneman concluded that being rich correlates with people spending less time doing things for fun and pleasure.

You don't have to copy them and risk burning out. You don't want to lose all work–life balance in your rush to become wealthy. But do bear in mind that if you choose to work 80 hours a week compared with a typical person's 40 hours, you could achieve in six months what others take a whole year to complete.

It comes down to your priorities and options. How important is it to you that you achieve the different goals in your life and how essential is it to take it easy and relax? Most people just want it too easy.

The wealthy are more likely to be behind their desks, on their computer or phone, than drinking cocktails or sun-bathing on the beach.

Put it into action

Decide the importance of your goals

Only you can decide how you spend your time and which of your life and financial goals should take priority. You'll be in a better position by now to measure what wealth means to you.

You can only accurately know how much effort is needed once you've jumped in and started. Like writing this book, I discovered how many hours I needed to invest only after I'd completed the first few pages.

Short-term pain for longer-term benefits

You're going to have to make sacrifices, at least in the short term, and that means being prepared to give up other activities, getting up earlier, spending less time watching Netflix and meeting friends. At the same time, find balance. Stop for regular exercise. Switch off on Sundays. There'll be more on this later.

Try to choose meaningful financial goals and activities

The secret to being able to work long hours without stress is purpose and meaning. Psychologist Mihaly Csikszentmihalyi calls this being in a state of 'flow' and it happens when you're doing things you love, that are aligned with your inner self. Find your 'flow' and everything seems effortless.

FACTS ARE FRIENDLY

'Look at reality – it is neither as you thought it was nor as you would like it to be.'

The truth can be so damn annoying when it doesn't back up the way you see the world. Sometimes turning a blind eye or putting your head in the sand feels like the only option, but ignoring the facts won't get you anywhere.

There are so many ways in which we can invest our money and allow ourselves to ignore reality. I have seen so many examples:

- We buy a house, only to discover that a large apartment block is going to be built behind it and we will lose our picturesque view and some property value. In truth we may have known about the planned development before buying but somehow went ahead anyway, perhaps telling ourselves, 'It will be OK'.
- We may invest in a friend's internet start-up, ignoring the fact that the founders have never succeeded in any of their previous business ventures. We should not be surprised that the start-up will probably fail.
- Perhaps we start a side business alongside our day job, in spite of knowing we do not have enough time to dedicate to both. We should not be surprised when the side business fails and performance in our day job worsens.

- We have a great business idea which we persist in pursuing, in spite of repeated advice to pull out and ignoring evidence that the idea is not particularly new, innovative or attractive to investors.

You can try ignoring the facts but they won't go away. The secret to financial success is to recognize unhealthy patterns and think before you make mistakes.

If you've invested money ignoring inconvenient truths, the facts will come back and bite you.

21

Put it into action

Know what you are basing decisions upon

Becoming wealthy involves making hundreds of decisions. You owe it to yourself and to your bank balance to ensure that all of them are well thought through, and that you've differentiated your ego, feelings, opinions and emotions from the facts and truths.

Psychologists have discovered that our thinking and actions are impacted by some very predictable cognitive bases. The following are the ones to watch out for as you make choices about where you put your time, trust and money:

- *Sunk cost fallacy*: this is where you become so emotionally invested in something that you lose the ability to be rational and accept that it hasn't worked out.
- *Selective perception*: this explains how easy it is to miss the full facts by focusing on a specific detail. Try watching the famous 'basketball and gorilla' video on YouTube. Most people don't spot the gorilla walking through the court while a match is taking place.
- *Anchoring bias*: this highlights the danger of over-reliance on the first information, opinions or facts you heard, causing you to ignore new information that appears later.
- *Confirmation bias*: this is where you only 'see' data that confirms what you want to be true because it aligns with what you want the answer to be.

Look out for such biases and how they influence you – especially when they could affect your decision making around money. You will never become wealthy by ignoring reality.

BE YOURSELF

'There is only one authentic you. Don't try to be like other people – you'll just end up a counterfeit version of them.'

It is always useful to study the habits, attitudes and mindsets of wealthy role models. There's so much to learn from how their wealth creation strategies and the business models they use have worked for them. Read their biographies for clues about how they succeeded and see which of their ideas, hints and tools you could borrow for yourself.

But the trick is not to do so blindly. A great technique for one person might be a disaster for you. Jack Dorsey, the billionaire co-founder of Twitter, follows the same routine every day with a daily morning ritual of getting up at 5 am, meditating for half an hour, before completing a fixed workout. Would you be financially successful if you did the same? You'd probably be fast asleep by midday. But the broad idea of following a fixed routine might serve you well.

So cut and paste what you see. Borrow selectively, and experiment with new ideas in your own context.

Be willing to adopt, experiment with and practise their habits, and through trial and error, you will find things that work for you.

22

Put it into action

Ask yourself, 'does it work for me?'

It's a safe bet that if someone's financially successful they've been doing something effective to achieve that. Make it your business to learn what other people have done and to understand their patterns and ways of working.

Just as importantly, you'll find things you aren't comfortable with. Plenty of people make a lot of money day trading, for example, but that doesn't mean it's for you. You *could* succeed financially that way, but do you actually want to trade stocks and bonds from your laptop?

Walk your own path

Getting wealthy means doing things *your* way, not becoming a carbon copy of those you're learning from. Experiment, take what's good, build on the ideas and habits you like, and ultimately tailor and tweak things to better you, your needs and situation.

YOUR REPUTATION IS EVERYTHING

'Live your life like you're being filmed 24/7.'

Your reputation is your brand. It's how others see you and judge your character. It's almost impossible to keep a great job, lead a successful start-up or attract investors if you have a poor reputation.

Global superstars like Tiger Woods and Lance Armstrong have lost sponsors because of reputational damage. Business leaders have had to resign over errors of judgement ranging from ill thought out social media posts to insider trading.

Wealth creation involves connecting and working with others, and your personal brand opens doors, whether it's senior colleagues fast tracking your career, your bank offering you financing, or a venture capital firm giving you start-up capital and expertise.

All of these people know that if they back you, their reputation will be intertwined with yours. If you fall, they are impacted, and no-one wants that. Be the safe bet, and people will always be there to support you.

It takes many years to build up your reputation and one moment to ruin it.

23

Put it into action

Protect your brand

You can make sure that your reputation is always good by watching your every word and action:

- Pause before sending emails, tweets or messages. Are you communicating exactly what you want to say or could it be misinterpreted?
- Think before making casual remarks. Is there any way your comments could be misconstrued as arrogant, discriminatory, sexist or bullying?
- Reflect before making any commitments and promises. Are you confident you can meet the expectations you have created?
- Be honest. We all tell lies – studies suggest we tell dozens of small and large lies every day. Aim for the truth and your reputation will benefit from it.

Be open

It's OK not to be perfect. Just aim to be open about your mistakes and weaknesses, whether it's the business start-up that failed, the job roles you struggled in, or coming clean and admitting that you don't know all the answers.

LEVERAGE YOUR MONEY WISELY

'When leverage is at play, a little becomes a lot. A small hill can be turned into a majestic mountain.'

It's very hard to get rich by only relying on your own money. Instead it's common for investors to borrow money, using the extra funds to buy assets such as properties, shares or businesses. Borrowing like this is referred to as leverage. It's not just about having more money, borrowing to invest also increases your percentage return on any investment. Let me show you this with an example of an investment property:

- You buy a $200,000 house using only $20,000 of your own money. You fund the remainder with a mortgage of $180,000.
- After one year the house's market price has risen by 10% so you choose to sell the property:

Proceeds of house sale	$220,000
Less repayment to bank	($180,000)
Profit from sale	$40,000

This gives you a return of 100% on the initial $20,000 you invested (i.e. you get back your initial $20,000 and make an additional $20,000).

This is the attraction of leverage. Had you used your own cash to pay the entire $200,000, you would only have made a 10% return – making a profit of $20,000, which is 10% more than you originally paid. We're ignoring fees and other costs because it's a simple example but you get the idea – borrowing money can give you a higher return on your investment.

The same multiplying of profit or return applies with other types of investments. Investors in the financial markets can trade a large position (e.g. buy a large number of shares or contracts) using only a small amount of your money or trading capital (i.e. margin).

Knowing how much to leverage your money takes careful thinking and practice.

24

Put it into action

Don't be greedy by over-leveraging

The power of leverage in good times is amazing. When the prices of stocks, shares, houses and other assets are rising, even the smallest investor can take home large profits compared with their initial upfront outlays. Borrowing to create a property empire or to become a trader in the financial markets can seem like easy money. It is no surprise that there are so many property mortgages. In the UK alone, there are over 11.1 million mortgages worth more than £1.4 trillion.

The danger comes when prices fall and you find yourself unable to pay off your borrowings from any available sales proceeds. In the example of the $200,000 house purchase, imagine if house prices fell by 20%. Your house is worth $160,000 and you owe the bank $180,000.

If this were your only problem investment, perhaps you could live with a $20,000 loss, but how do you cope if you have bought four other properties, all relying on similar bank loans? Do you hold onto them, hoping they rise in value, or do you sell and make a large loss? How would you repay the bank the full amount owed?

You have to be careful about how many assets, of any kind, you buy with borrowed money. Too much leveraging is the easiest and fastest way for you to lose all of your wealth. Don't let the good times fool you into thinking your investments will never lose value. Always ask yourself if you can survive a downturn in the value of your leveraged investments.

NO WHITE FLAGS

'Never give up. Most people never reach the peak of the mountain, and give up at the slightest incline.'

According to Credit Suisse, over 99.5% of us are *not* millionaires. Of the 42 million millionaires in the world, the majority have only achieved that status because their homes have risen in value. Making money is a long, hard, unclear and lonely path and there are many reasons to throw in the towel along the way.

Everywhere you look, people are facing setbacks:

- 43% of Americans feel 'they are not even close' to achieving financial independence, according to a 2017 poll by Consolidated Credit, Inc.
- One third of Australian pensioners are living in poverty, according to a 2016 study by Per Capita think tank.
- 48% of British investors are failing to achieve their financial goals, according to a 2018 survey by the research firm FTI and syndicateroom.com.

Becoming rich may not be everything, but achieving your financial goals is surely important enough not to give up at the first setback?

You've started this and you need to finish it. Giving up is not an option.

Put it into action

Keep on walking

Make sure your financial goals are really important to you. If you truly believe that your goals are essential, then it'll be harder for you to give up on them.

Celebrate short-term achievements

Recognize your successes and any hurdles you've overcome, no matter how small. This will help remind you that success is possible, that the bigger picture can happen, and that you can reach your main goals.

Develop persistence

This is not easy. Some people are naturally more persistent than others. So how do you become more persistent?

- Slow down and be patient. If you don't expect everything instantly, you'll be better able to stay the course.
- Pause before reacting to events and situations. When you feel like throwing in the towel, go home and sleep on it. Come back to the challenge fresh in the morning.
- Surround yourself with support. Just having people to talk to who will encourage you to stay on track can help.

View everything as a lesson

Expect delays, roadblocks, financial setbacks and mistakes. Everything is a lesson and if you look hard enough it will show you:

- How to avoid a repeat
- What to do differently
- Where to change your actions, behaviours and plans.

DON'T GET SENTIMENTAL

'You don't have to sell your grandmother. She can stay. But everything else must go!'

It's only human to become attached to things you've had for some time and the same applies to investments. But just because it's your baby doesn't make it great. You should never get emotionally attached to your investments – and you have to always be willing to let go when the time's right. Too many investors struggle to walk away.

My grandfather held onto his shop in Yorkshire in the UK for decades. It was a business he'd created from scratch and he turned down great financial offers to sell it, in spite of signs it was in decline as supermarkets appeared all around. He was reluctant to let go, and when he did finally sell, it was for a fraction of what he could have got if he'd sold earlier.

Developing an emotional attachment to your money or investments because they connect you to your past, or for some other reason, is just sentimental.

Let your babies go when the time comes or you'll end up with under-performing 'adults'.

Put it into action

Get over your attachment issues

Look at your finances, work obligations and investments and think about why you acquired each of them, asking yourself, 'why am I still holding onto them?'

- Do you have company stocks and shares just because your first job was with them?
- Are you soldiering on with an inherited family business because pulling the plug would mean giving up on your parents' dreams?
- Are you ploughing more funds into a loss-making real estate business because you've put so much heart and soul into it you can't bear to let go?

You don't have to sell an asset or investment just because you have an emotional attachment to it – you just need to get rid of any you're keeping *because of* the emotional attachment.

Cut the cord

It's human to have emotional bonds and connections, but if they are causing your wealth to fall, you have to decide between the importance of meeting your financial goals and holding onto your past.

GIVE AND YOU WILL RECEIVE

'You can't carry all of your wealth with you. You have to give some to others.'

According to a study by researchers at the University of Zurich published in the journal *Nature Communications* in 2017, even when only donating small amounts, your happiness, satisfaction and well-being improve to the same degree as if you'd given away much larger sums of money. Get into the habit of giving to those in need on a regular basis. As well as helping others, you'll be helping yourself.

The other benefit to you is that when you give, even without any expectation of anything in return, you will receive back. In a 2007 study titled '*Altruism and Indirect Reciprocity*', sociologists Brent Simpson and Robb Willer demonstrated that it's highly likely that your generosity today will be rewarded later. Generosity increases your altruistic reputation and this increases the likelihood of you receiving future benefits in return from third parties, even people who haven't benefited from your own giving.

This may all sound like weak science, but it mirrors many spiritual and religious teachings. The Hindu and Buddhist faiths talk about karma, Christianity talks about 'reaping what you sow' and 'give and you will receive'. Outside of religion, people talk about the energy in the universe and the law of attraction. Whatever your perspective, there seems to be something in it.

Keep an open mind – being generous can create an environment of generosity around you.

Put it into action

Keep an open mind

You might be very comfortable with the idea that positive giving creates an energy of abundance around you. You might believe in the idea of karma, in which good deeds will come back to us in some way. The suggestion that we create our own positive reality through projecting positive energy might also appeal to you. This topic is covered in many best-selling self-help books, such as Rhonda Byrne's *The Secret* and Wayne Dyer's *The Power of Intention*. Allow yourself to go along with the idea that being generous can create an environment of generosity around you.

Start today

Don't wait until you're super wealthy or retired. Why would you want to wait years before giving back? Start today.

Start small

Give what you can today and don't feel guilty if it's just small sums. Donating small amounts to a charity is a perfect start. Later, as you build up your wealth, you can choose to give away larger amounts or even consider bequeathing money in your will to charitable causes. And don't forget the tax benefits of giving to registered charities.

COMPOUND INTEREST IS MAGIC

'Discover the joys of compound interest. Understand it and it will make you rich. Misunderstand it and it will make you poor.'

Compound interest can make or break you. Depositing money in a savings account and leaving it untouched over many years can yield a small fortune, but an unpaid credit card bill can drag you down.

Even with low interest rates, the impact of compounding is significant. Let me demonstrate this with a little maths. Imagine you've been given $1,000 that you place in a new savings account that pays you, before tax, 3% interest per year. You leave the account untouched. Watch how the balance grows as annual interest is calculated on the full balance at the end of each year.

Year 1	$1,030	Year 6	$1,194
Year 2	$1,061	Year 7	$1,230
Year 3	$1,093	Year 8	$1,267
Year 4	$1,126	Year 9	$1,305
Year 5	$1,159	Year 10	$1,344

Even at a low deposit interest rate of 3%, your money has grown by a third over ten years. This is the joy of earning interest on interest, or compounding.

The flipside is the hit you'll get from leaving your debts unpaid. Like everything, compound interest can work for you or against you if you're not wise to it.

Don't underestimate small amounts of interest. It all adds up over time.

28

Put it into action

Avoid paying compound interest

The interest rates you pay are always higher than the deposit rates you receive. You can use the low interest rates on some types of loan to your advantage but the interest on credit card bills and payday loans is always damaging and the effects of high compound interest working against you can be frightening.

Even with government limits, you could easily be paying over 30% annual interest – sometimes referred to as the APR, which stands for the annual percentage rate. It is often very hard to know how much you'll be charged until you receive your monthly bill from your bank. Sometimes interest is calculated daily, which can make the total amounts payable higher.

This example shows how a small unpaid credit card bill can mushroom into enormous debt. Let's assume that none of the balance is paid off and that you borrow $1,000 in December. Interest is charged for the first time in January. The APR is 24%, with interest calculated monthly:

- January – interest is 2% of $1,000, which is $20
- February – interest is 2% of $1,020, which is $20.40
- March – interest is 2% of $1,040.40, which is $20.80
- By December, you would need to pay £1,243.37 to clear your total balance, excluding any other fees that you may be charged. Next time you delay paying back money, be aware of how much it might cost you.

With payday loans you might end up owing much more, as high as two or three times the original amount borrowed.

Start small and be patient

When you can, set aside some spare funds in a savings account to earn compound interest. Only withdraw funds if you have a more productive use lined up such as buying bonds or property or investing in a business. Otherwise just sit back and watch the balance grow.

PREDICTABLE INCOME GIVES YOU PEACE OF MIND

'Give me a permanent income, and I will be at peace.'

In our volatile and ever-changing world, earning a reliable and regular income is a blessing that allows you to concentrate on building your wealth, instead of worrying about where your next meal is coming from. If you can forecast your money coming in with any accuracy, then you are in a strong position.

Recurring, or residual, income continues to flow to you after the work has been done and as a rule of thumb it comes from two sources:

1. The returns and income on assets that you own
2. Income generated through businesses and work you undertake.

If you have money coming in from any of the following, you are earning residual income:

- A salary or wage
- Deposit interest on your savings account
- Rental income on your properties, including Airbnb holiday lets
- Selling products and services – you may have a regular volume of business, or even better, customers might subscribe for your services
- A network marketing business
- Dividends and returns on your investment portfolio
- Royalties and fees payable to you for your patents and ideas, including books you have written.

These are the building blocks of your wealth, and we'll be learning more about them and how to maximize them throughout the book.

Having certainty over at least some of your income flows can take the stress out of increasing your wealth.

29

Put it into action

Use a recurring income stream as a springboard

You should regard any regular recurring income as a cushion or insurance; you know it's coming in, leaving you free to explore other options for growing your financial wealth and achieving your goals. It will allow you to take a few risks with your money, to experiment, learn and try out new investment and income generation ideas.

Seek automatic recurring income

The ideal recurring income is passive income. This is money you earn while you're sleeping and requires little or none of your time and effort to create and maintain. There'll be more on this later.

Don't take your eye off the ball

No income flow is truly automatic or 100% guaranteed. Just because it's regular and recurrent does not mean you can forget about it. All income flows require some level of attention and support, so be observant and keep an eye on all your sources of wealth.

- If you own rental properties in a particular town, keep an eye on the area. Watch out for new developments that might impact the value and attractiveness of your houses or apartments.
- Keep an eye out for changing tax rules that may have an impact on your investments and potentially make them more or less attractive to hold.
- Don't blindly trust the people who manage the assets that produce your recurring income. No property agent, stockbroker or fund manager is perfect.

PAY OFF UNPRODUCTIVE DEBTS

'Debt can twist even the happiest person.'

If you're drowning in debt and struggling to make ends meet, you need to decide if your debt is productive or unproductive.

Some debt is helpful. This is your productive debt – the borrowings taken out to help you invest in property or fund other investments, including help to buy or grow a business. These investments give you rental and dividend incomes. They produce income flows that should hopefully cover the interest charged on the initial borrowings.

Your unproductive consumer debts are the ones that should worry you. Have you totalled up all of your credit cards, hire purchase payments, payday loans, car loans and bank overdrafts yet? These are the debts that can cripple you with their high fees and interest payments and with no income flows being generated from the money borrowed.

Large unproductive debts will hold you back from becoming wealthy. In fact they'll make you poor, depressed and anxious.

30

Put it into action

Prioritize your debts

List everything you owe, including the amounts and monies borrowed. Include the potentially productive debts, such as any mortgages, and list those unproductive debts such as credit card bills and loan repayments. Include all your financial obligations, including monthly instalments. Establish in particular if you have any debts that could lead to legal action or further financial penalties if they're not repaid.

Analyse the costs

How much interest are you being charged on the money you owe? Try to work out what the fees are and if there are any fees attached to early repayment. The goal is to understand which debts are more expensive and which to repay faster to minimize your total outgoings. Note where there are tax benefits from certain payments, for example on mortgage interest payments in the UK.

Reduce the cost of your debt

This can be achieved in many ways, including:

- using any extra cash to pay off certain debts
- re-negotiating debts, including your mortgage
- taking out cheaper forms of borrowing and using funds to pay off your higher cost debt.

Debt is a difficult subject and if you are having serious problems, you should seek help and advice. In the UK, there are many avenues to turn to, including the Citizen's Advice Bureau and the Money Charity. In the US there are similar services available such as those offered by Debt. org and the National Foundation for Credit Counseling.

DON'T GAMBLE

'If you want to gamble, throw this book away. Take your savings to Las Vegas or Macau and enjoy them while they last.'

The wealthy generally don't gamble. In a US study by author and financial planner Thomas Corley, 77% of the poor admitted to regularly playing the lottery compared with only 6% of the wealthy. Corley's take-away was that the poor '*are relying on random good luck to bail them out in life rather than the opportunity luck that the rich rely on*'. Opportunity luck is the kind of luck you need to focus on creating (we'll cover this later).

Don't think gambling is just about casinos, betting shops and lottery tickets either. There have been plenty of blind rushes on the stock market over the years where investors have scrambled to buy and sell for a profit on the back of an investing frenzy without any idea what they're doing, only to get their fingers burned.

Of course some lucky person is going to scoop the lottery, but the probability of it being you is infinitesimal. Much better to put your money in situations you can control, or at least have more control over, investing in income-generating assets, rather than hoping that lady luck is smiling on you.

No one ever got wealthy waiting for a winning streak.

Put it into action

Avoid gambling

Everyone likes a flutter but gambling doesn't pay and you won't become a successful investor through luck. Never buy shares, options, derivatives, properties and other assets purely based on your feelings, good fortune or a whim. It doesn't matter if you've seen others become wealthy through speculating. Unless you understand the market you're investing in, you should steer clear.

The rules for eliminating gambling from your investments are:

- Always study the opportunities you want to invest in, be it the housing market, shares in a newly listed company or becoming a co-founder of a start-up.
- Try to invest small amounts to start with no matter how amazing the opportunity sounds.
- Never throw all your money into any single venture or investment.

Just don't ...

Steer well clear of betting websites, where the algorithms are designed to ensure that, on average, the website wins and not you. The odds are stacked against you. The probability of winning is incredibly low. Bet for fun using spare change, never with the intention of becoming wealthy.

DON'T BORROW FROM ANYONE CLOSE

'What's more important – their friendship or their money?'

Taking out loans to build up your income-generating assets is part and parcel of growing your wealth and family and friends can seem like an obvious source of funds:

- They're easy to find and connect with.
- They know you, and you know them.
- You can guess how kind and generous they'll be.
- You may already know how much cash they have in their bank accounts.
- They may understand what you're trying to achieve and appreciate why you need money.

By contrast, banks, professional investors and other potential sources of money are more complicated and demanding. There's paperwork, business plans, guarantees, loan documentation, due diligence reports … They need time to become acquainted with you, to understand why you need funding and to work through their processes. And at the end of all that, their financial analyses and risk assessments might conclude that they can't give you as much as you need.

Despite all that, it's best, where possible, not to rely on your nearest and dearest. People can feel pressured to help you, but worried that you won't repay on time, or that you won't pay them interest or sign a loan agreement. Remember your Shakespeare and think twice before you test your friendships and family bonds.

'Loan oft loses both itself and friend.' (William Shakespeare)

Put it into action

Exhaust other sources first

Before approaching your mum or best friend, be sure you've exhausted all other sources. If banks, professional investors and other sources of funds aren't willing to lend to you, try to understand the issues:

- They might feel your plans are too small.
- They might think you lack the collateral to offer in return.
- You might have a poor credit history, or no secure income to give them confidence they can entrust their money to you.

If the professionals won't lend to you, is it even OK asking those close to you? Think about whether the bank's concerns are valid and why they see you as a high-risk borrower before you turn to friends and family.

If you must ...

If your last resort is to borrow from those around you, follow these tips:

- Never compel someone to lend to you.
- Don't negotiate too much.
- Be sure they have spare money, and are comfortable lending it.
- Talk about worst case scenarios and how you will both deal with you having repayment difficulties.
- Offer and agree to pay a market level of interest rate.
- Have a written agreement that both parties sign, along with a neutral witness.
- Pay off the loan as soon as you can, and faster than you promised.
- Be very thankful, and be willing to help in return one day.

TAKE SOME RISKS

'The most dangerous risk is not to take one.'

Becoming wealthy involves risks. As a rule of thumb, the higher the potential return from an asset or investment, the higher the risk of that return not being achieved. Typically, the probability of fluctuations in the amount of return increases with higher return investments.

At one end of the spectrum you can leave your money in a high street bank and receive a very small, but 100% assured, rate of interest. At the other extreme are tech start-up companies with high failure rates where the high risk of losing your money is offset by potentially large returns for the lucky few who see their investments repaid 100 times over after the firm goes to IPO and lists on a stock exchange.

There is no totally safe way of increasing your net worth. The probabilities might vary, but anything with a financial value can fall:

- Share prices can lose value, or worse, the company can go bankrupt.
- House prices can fall, or a property can lose value due to subsidence or new developments nearby.
- All manner of financial products, from derivatives to forex swaps, can lose you money, become worthless, or worse, cost you money.
- Gold, US Treasury Bills, UK gilts and other supposedly safe haven assets can fall in value.
- Cash can seem safe, but high inflation can make its true value fall.
- Physical assets such as artwork can be stolen or damaged.

If you want wealth, you will have to take some risks.

Put it into action

How much time do you have?

Your level of risk tolerance (or threshold) will vary depending on whether you're planning to retire in one year or in 20 years' time. The more time you have to grow your wealth, the more opportunity you have to pursue higher returns with a greater level of risk. If you fail, you still have time to recoup losses.

Conversely, if you have fewer years to grow your wealth, you should take more care. Be cautious about putting any of your money into high-risk investments: 3% fixed deposit interest from your local bank at this point might start to appear very attractive.

Explore your tolerance for risk

Are you a natural risk taker, or are you risk averse? If you normally play it safe you might need to come out of your comfort zone, and if you're very bullish and readily jump into risks, you might need to hold back sometimes.

Risk-weight your investments

This might sound a little technical, but the idea is very simple. The goal is to hold a mixture of investments, some with a high return and high-risk combination, others with a more guaranteed but lower return. If your desired investment portfolio is varied and complex, seek the help of a financial advisor, private banker or accountant to help you create a suitable balance of high- and low-risk investments.

WATCH OUT FOR CURRENCY SWINGS

'What goes up always comes down … but never when you expect it.'

You can lose the shirt off your back when an exchange rate turns against you. I once knew someone who owned a large apartment in Hong Kong. Eyeing the very low interest rates in Japan, a mortgage advisor encouraged him to switch his mortgage from Hong Kong dollars (HK$) to Japanese yen. His monthly mortgage payments dropped overnight and all was good until the following year when the yen appreciated against the HK$. Suddenly he had to find more HK$ to convert to pay yen to meet his monthly mortgage payments. The yen strengthened so much that he found himself having to pay much more than if he had simply remained with a HK$ mortgage.

Many people are enticed by 'money saving' opportunities, but there is so much potential for things to go wrong. In a world where currencies and exchange rates are constantly moving up and down it is impossible to predict with 100% accuracy how they will move over time. It's perfectly possible to have an asset (home) and income flow (salary and rental income) in one currency (e.g. HK$ or £), and a debt or obligation (mortgage loan) in another (e.g. yen or Swiss franc) – but you can never predict if you will gain or lose out over time.

The same risks lie with businesses that sell overseas (i.e. they export) and/or buy raw materials and services from overseas (i.e. they import). If you are investing in or running such a business, you need to be aware of the currency risks. Imports can become more expensive when your own currency weakens (depreciates), while your sales revenue falls when your currency rises (appreciates).

Similarly, there are risks when investing your money in foreign-currency denominated funds and financial products. If your own currency depreciates, the investment is worth less when converted back.

If in doubt keep your money in your own local currency.

34

Put it into action

Control your urges

Take care with great deals involving different countries and currencies. Your CPA or IFA might pitch the lower interest rates in a different country, or higher financial returns, but exercise caution.

Keep it simple and do matching

As a rule of thumb, ensure that any assets, and loans on those assets, are both in the same currency as the income sources to be used to pay off those loans. This is called matching and can avoid much heartache.

In cases where you need to invest, buy or sell overseas, you can practise foreign currency hedging. At its most simple, this involves paying a fee to your bank to buy a foreign currency at a pre-determined fixed exchange rate. Alternatively, you can buy any needed foreign currency earlier than required if the exchange rate is in your favour and 'lock in' at a known exchange rate. In a small way, this is what you do already when you buy foreign currency for your annual vacation weeks or months before you actually travel.

Understand the maths involved with exchange rate movements

Rising and falling currencies are confusing. At the time of writing, US$1.00 equals £0.78. This means £1.00 equals US$1.28. When US dollars depreciate against a currency (e.g. sterling), this means it equals less in sterling (e.g. US$1 falls to £0.68 from earlier, equalling £0.78). When it appreciates, the opposite happens and each US dollar is worth more in sterling. For example, US$1.00 moves from being equivalent to £0.78 and rises to perhaps equal £0.88. Make sure your understanding of rates is solid before you enter into any deal or investment.

KEEP OWNERSHIP

'When you give up ownership, you are giving up your freedom for a short-term gain.'

No matter how desperate you are for extra funding, try not to give away shareholdings, either in a business or a share of assets you own, such as property or even a wine collection. If you do, you will have to share all the future profits, sales proceeds and success in the years to come.

There are plenty of cautionary tales of people who have taken investments from business acquaintances when they've reached a dead end with the banks. One person I know gave two acquaintances each 25% of their company's shares to fund the business' growth. The business has now grown into a multi-million-dollar company and the investors, who have little involvement in it, enjoy 50% of the spoils.

Be careful of giving up control. If you give up a large percentage of your shares, you will no longer be able to make decisions alone and will be unable to act without someone else's approval and agreement. You may come to resent how much you gave up for what, with hindsight, might seem like a small investment.

Will you regret having given away the shareholding in your business?

35

Put it into action

Look for alternative financing

Giving away ownership should be your last resort. Before you go there explore:

- taking out a loan – but beware of high interest 'loan shark' offerings. The ideal is funding from a well-known financial institution
- other forms of financing. Perhaps your clients could pay you faster or your suppliers give you longer credit terms if you negotiate and offer incentives.

Note that mortgage financing involves a bank or building society taking rights or a lien over your home. The bank doesn't automatically own your new home but they have the legal recourse to do so. This is quite different to giving someone, upfront and permanently, a percentage of your company's shares in return for funds to grow your business or keep it afloat.

Negotiate hard

If you really must give up shares in return for money, keep to an absolute minimum the amount of shareholding you relinquish. Aim to agree a high value for your company's shares. Think about how you will feel in the future about what you agree today. It might even be better to walk away and in extreme cases close down your business, rather than work with a new major shareholder.

Have a buy-back clause in your agreement

Try to negotiate the right to buy back the shares you're giving away in any new shareholder agreement. Agree upfront how the price of the shares (in the future) will be calculated and agreed.

DON'T COUNT YOUR CHICKENS

'Don't sell the bags of crisps before you have picked and peeled the potatoes.'

Beware of counting paper profits, signed contracts with clients, unrealized investment gains and other unpaid income as real money and wealth. Your actual realized money and returns might be much lower, delayed or even become impossible to materialize. Remember:

- Not every client pays all of its suppliers on time or in full.
- Contracts might only be as good as the paper they're written on.
- Your offer of a new job on a high salary might be withdrawn.
- Investment gains on paper can disappear overnight.
- Profits on paper may not translate into money in your hands.

Never treat the amounts payable to you as real cash and use it before you actually have it.

A business that you're a founder of, or shareholder in, might be very profitable but also heavily in debt with no cash in the bank. It's very common to have negative cashflow and it can occur for many reasons:

- Customers not paying on time
- Too much money tied up in unsold stocks
- Large investments made in unproductive assets.

If you're a shareholder of a highly profitable company you might feel wealthy, but it'll be a different story if the business is so heavily indebted it's forced to go into liquidation to pay off its creditors.

> If the income stream has not arrived, never commit to spending it.

36

Put it into action

Don't spend or use money that's not 100% guaranteed

Take care not to make plans and commitments that involve money you don't yet have your hands on such as:

- money owed to you by a client or a friend
- dividends payable from a business you own that delays paying due to cashflow issues
- a new job contract that's not yet signed or a new job you haven't yet begun.

Life is fragile, things change, people make false promises and play games. Don't risk being left high and dry with commitments you can't meet. Don't celebrate a great new job with a fancy car, only to have your contract terminated after the probation period.

- Avoid rushing. Pause, be patient and, if in doubt, wait.
- Never become greedy or show off.
- Be certain that you have all the funds before using them in any way.

BUILD BRIDGES

'Wealthy people look to earn relationships and networks. Everybody else simply looks to earn a pay cheque.'

When was the last time you met someone for the very first time? Getting people on your side can transform your wealth prospects. In his autobiography, Eugene O'Kelly, the late chairman of the global accountancy group Ernst & Young, recounts the story of being so determined to meet a key client prospect that he actually had his assistant book him a flight ticket and specific seat, just to be able to sit next to the potential client.

Some people will stop at nothing to engineer a chance encounter. So think about the type of people who could help you. They're likely to:

- be successful and wealthy and someone you can learn from
- have a very positive 'anything is possible' mindset and be able to help your better qualities and traits come out
- have expertise and be a source of ideas and advice on topics you need
- have an amazing network of contacts that you could be introduced to in the future.

You might find the prospect of reaching out to strangers daunting or feel uncomfortable connecting with new people. It's definitely not easy and it takes practice, but if you feel it's important enough, you'll be able to do it.

Networks have power, and nurturing and growing yours is one of the best things you can do in your quest to build wealth.

37

Put it into action

First impressions count

If you're an extrovert it might be natural to spend time connecting with people, but it's not so simple if you're a quiet introvert. In that case, think through and practise how you might introduce yourself, how you'll describe what you are trying to achieve and how to bring up the topic of what help and support you want.

Attend useful functions and events

What kinds of networking events could you attend? The following are some ideas for starters:

- Networking events of successful investors and entrepreneurs, such as the YPO (formerly called the Young Professionals Organisation)
- Industry-specific expos
- Chambers of Commerce events
- Courses and workshops in different aspects of creating wealth.

Make it a two-way relationship

When making a new connection, think about what you can offer them in return. Start asking people how you can help them and what you can do to support them. I often provide coaching and leadership advice and you'll have skills you can offer too.

Don't lose touch

Once you've built new bridges, don't allow them to fall apart. Make an effort to maintain your connections, allowing yourself to become professional friends.

INVEST IN BRICKS AND MORTAR

'I like real estate. I can see it, feel and touch it. Someone always wants to live or work in it.'

It's highly likely that you'll either make your wealth through property or you'll make money elsewhere and use it to buy property. Wealthy people throughout the world all own property as part of their portfolio of assets.

Property comes in many forms – individual houses and apartments, entire residential developments or buildings, commercial property including land, shop lots, office towers, factories and warehouses.

Why is it so popular with the wealthy?

- Property prices normally rise over time (although of course they can fall, usually caused by an economic downturn, an over-supply and/or a bursting property price bubble).
- Property comes in all forms and sizes and is found everywhere, with something to suit all tastes and budgets, from expensive mansions through to low cost student housing.
- Rental income is normally a good percentage return on the property's value. It is also a reliable form of passive income (of which you'll learn more later).
- Like gold, property is a physical asset that doesn't easily disappear – at least not unless a natural disaster such as an earthquake or tsunami strikes. Physical assets can seem safer than paper investments. In countries such as the US and the UK, property investments are protected by very good land rights. It's hard for someone to steal your house or factory.
- Financing for help to buy property is readily available in at least all of the world's developed economies. As a result, you can buy a property without needing to pay upfront 100% of the property's asking price.
- There's a ready market for buying and selling properties in most countries.
- You can live in and/or work within a property you own.

Investing in property is one of the most common ways of creating wealth.

38

Put it into action

Build up a property empire, one brick at a time

Start small with a studio apartment if necessary, but start today, buying whatever you can afford. Better to have a foot on the property ladder now than to enter it later when prices may have risen. As well as buying a home to live in, you could start buying second or third properties with bank financing that can be rented out, with the rental income hopefully more than covering your monthly mortgage repayments and other expenses that you have to cover as a landlord.

Location, location, location

Buy in the right locations. With my own property investments, those in great locations have always appreciated in value and sold quickly.

Shop around for great financing deals

Your challenge is to save sufficient money to be able to pay a deposit as well as cover other purchase costs. The sooner you can start saving up for a deposit the better. Unless you are flush with cash, it is wise to have a bank help you purchase a property. You only need to come up with a small percentage, such as 10%, of the purchase price.

Obtaining a bank loan or mortgage is not difficult. In countries such as the US and UK, there are numerous financial institutions offering property loans or mortgages and there are some excellent websites, such as www.moneysupermarket.com (UK) or www.bankrate.com (US) where you can compare the available offerings. Be careful with your choice of mortgage, and be especially careful of interest-only mortgages, where you do not regularly repay the capital amount.

How can the government help you?

In the UK, take advantage of any government schemes such as the UK's first-time buyer programmes: Help to Buy, Right to Buy and Shared Ownership. In the US, housing loans for first-time buyers are available from the Federal Housing Administration. Such loans are viewed as easier to obtain and less strict in terms of requirements compared with banks. Other countries have similar schemes such as Singapore's cheaper HDB apartments.

EASY COME, EASY GO

'From a life of poverty back to a life of poverty in three generations.'

The majority of people who inherit wealth lose it. According to the US-based wealth consultancy Williams Group, 70% of wealthy families have lost all their wealth by the second generation, and 90% by the third. It is a similar story for those who win the lottery – far too many let it slip through their fingers, spending it all within a couple of years.

Money that arrives in your lap without any effort is hard to manage and many people in this situation just don't understand the idea of using the money as capital from which you can earn income. At least with an inheritance you may have seen your parents working hard to earn and maintain the money, so you have a bit of a head start in terms of valuing wealth.

Sadly, many of us aren't prepared for receiving an inheritance, often because our parents don't trust us and/or don't sufficiently prepare us. This is reflected in a 2015 survey by the American private bank US Trust which found that:

- 78% of respondents said their children were not financially responsible enough to handle an inheritance
- 64% had disclosed very little or nothing at all about their wealth to their children.

It's no surprise that so many countries have cultural stories about the wealth being squandered by children and grandchildren.

Do you really want to work hard to create wealth knowing that your offspring will lose it all?

Put it into action

Learn from your parents

If you're hoping to inherit wealth, take an interest in how your parents create, maintain and grow what they own. Observe, ask and understand how they manage everything. This might include their properties, share portfolios, relationships with their banks, taxation issues, offshore trusts and whatever else is involved with their wealth.

Offer to help your parents so that you can get an appreciation of the challenges involved. Ask to attend key meetings with them, or in their place, for example, with a bank's relationship manager, stockbroker, tax accountant or property manager.

Be financially skilled

The secret to successfully inheriting wealth is to have the right knowledge and skills. You have to know what you don't know as well as what you do know. You have to appreciate the need for expert help and advice and consider taking courses in finance and wealth management.

Treat the money as if you had sweated and toiled to earn it

Adopting the right mindset isn't easy. If you're lucky, your parents will have brought you up with the right money mindset so you know to pause before you act, spend wisely and never invest recklessly. If you don't have these qualities, then reading this book and practising its contents will help you before you come into any money.

SHOW GRATITUDE

'Never forget those who gave you a leg up. You never know when you'll need each other again.'

The difference between financial success and failure can be wafer thin and the outcome can be swayed by the slightest help from just one person. Some of today's billionaires still talk about pivotal moments in their lives that often hinged on a simple gesture. The Hong Kong-based multi-billionaire Li Ka-Shing is now one of the world's richest people with a vast empire of businesses and properties, but back in the 1950s he was simply a manufacturer of plastic flowers who has spoken of being really helped by a particular supplier who extended payment terms to him.

We can all find examples of people who helped us get where we are, whether it's just guidance with a first job or investment advice. It's never easy in the early days when you don't have the money or the knowledge. Showing gratitude and letting people know how significant a role they've played in your life is good for you, and good for the person who gave you the leg up.

Who has helped you and who could you help in turn?

40

Put it into action

Acknowledge people who help you today

You may not yet have met the person who will open doors for you, but when you do, be ready to give thanks and keep in touch. Try to reciprocate in any way you can. One of my key clients has passed me much business over the years and I was able to reciprocate in unexpected ways – giving his children advice on studying and careers. Be grateful and demonstrate gratitude and recognize that you have no idea how and why your paths may cross again in the future.

Keep in touch with people who helped you in the past

What goes around comes around. Consciously keep in touch even if it's just on social media (Facebook, LinkedIn, Instagram and Twitter) or by sharing articles and ideas via WhatsApp and email. You will find that by doing this you will end up helping them, and equally enjoying their help again, sometimes in incredible ways.

CLEAN UP YOUR PAST

'Take great care of your credit, and it will take great care of you.'

If there's anything in your past that might be holding you back from financial success, address it head on. These examples are more common than you would think:

- Poor credit history. Years of unpaid credit card bills can come back to haunt you, creating problems applying for loans and mortgages long after the event.
- Ill-advised social media posts. Don't be pigeonholed by things you've posted in the past, especially if they could be deemed offensive and unwise. It will certainly affect your prospects.
- An airbrushed CV. Make sure your career details are correct as far as you can. Inaccuracy about past salary levels, job titles held or dates spent in particular job roles will be found out and raise questions about your credibility.

Some things you can't change – if you have a legal summons or related police matters on record, there's really not much you can do – but make sure you're on top of everything in your control and that you present a consistent face to the world.

Skeletons never stay shut in the closet.

41

Put it into action

Clean up your credit history to borrow cheaper

Get yourself on the electoral roll to be sure of being able to get a mortgage. If you don't have any borrowing history, getting a mortgage may be difficult, and if you do get one, you may have to pay higher interest. To get some credit history, use a credit card and make sure you pay off the full balance each month. In the UK, it's possible to include your rent in your credit file through the Rental Exchange Initiative; go to sites such as experian.co.uk or capitalone.co.uk to check your credit ratings and to check if you think they're accurate. In the US go to www.creditsesame.com, www.creditkarma.com or www.Experian.com. If not, you can submit online credit report queries.

Clean up your online history

Don't let your years online come back to bite you. Review all of your past social media posts, including your entire Facebook history right down to those 'Likes' for posts that, on re-reading, you realize might embarrass you. Think about making your past posts private and de-activating some of your social media accounts.

Be honest on your CV

If you've exaggerated your past job titles and responsibilities or hidden periods of unemployment on your CV, edit it to show the truth. If you didn't actually finish the degree or course you started, just get the truth out there. You're old enough now to come clean.

Tackle legal issues

If there are legal matters that can be cleaned up, get it done. This is easier said than done of course in some instances, but if there's some kind of claim or lien against you that can be removed, take steps to do it.

MAKE FAILURE YOUR BEST FRIEND

'Success is always awaiting you, beyond the horizon of failures.'

Every year hundreds of people set out to conquer Everest knowing that they may return without having stood on the summit. According to the Himalayan Database, as of December 2017, only 4,833 mountaineers have ever reached the top. In 2017 39% failed and 288 people have died on the mountain between 1922 and 2017. Does this stop people trying?

Becoming wealthy can be as challenging as climbing Mount Everest. The road to building up your financial assets and returns is fraught with dangers and filled with the very real possibility of failure: house prices fall, companies go into liquidation, mutual funds collapse in value.

Examples of failure are everywhere, but like the committed climber, stay focused on your goal. Learn what you can from it and move on.

Many mountaineers who didn't conquer Everest first time round return to base camp for another attempt, and many who failed on their first attempt finally get the ultimate prize because they refused to stop trying.

42

Put it into action

Own your fears

It's human to fear. It dates back to our time in caves when death was a daily possibility and we were honing our 'flight or fight' instincts. Successful people all have fears that they counter with lots of courage and determination.

There are three important and related questions you need to ask to help you evaluate how to proceed with a financial investment:

1. *What are you afraid of losing?* Be objective and honest. It doesn't matter if your fears seem small or insignificant. Don't be embarrassed if you sense they're trivial.
2. *What would you be missing out on?* By not proceeding with an investment or financial opportunity, what upsides and returns will you miss? How important is that income to you?
3. *What's the worst that can happen?* If you pursue a financial investment and your worst fears are realized, what is the real impact on your bank balance, total wealth and plan to achieve your dreams?

Reduce the risk of catastrophic failure

Overcoming your fear of failure doesn't mean ignoring risks. There should never be a scenario where you might lose everything. There are many ways of avoiding a catastrophe like this, including learning how to manage your risks, understanding the dangers of having all your wealth in one basket, and taking advice on protecting your investments.

CREATE YOUR OWN LUCK

'Luck is a simple dish, made up of some very simple ingredients – planning, determination and hard work.'

Wealthy people tend to be lucky people. But there's a pattern of good fortune in very successful people that goes deeper than just a random lottery win. They tend to consistently get lucky breaks, or find themselves in the right place at the right time, like the investor who happens to get invited into a tech start-up from day one or the share trader who sells his shares in a company, just before the share price collapses.

Richard Wiseman is a professor of psychology who has studied luck and found that how lucky you are relates to how much effort you put into noticing and acting on chances and opportunities. Which is exactly what wealthy people do. They put themselves into situations where they're more likely to get a lucky break. They create opportunities and are ready to take advantage of them.

It turns out that being lucky comes down to hard work, and using your initiative, intuition and intelligence.

43

Put it into action

Get out more

What opportunities do you need to create to achieve your lucky breaks? I was 'lucky' enough to have renowned business coach and author Marshall Goldsmith write a foreword to my last book. That happened because I sought him out and spent time getting to know him. Who do you need to meet and what events do you need to attend where you could create that opportunity?

Nothing is too crazy when it comes to pursuing lucky breaks. All it takes is some innovative thinking to create the opportunity. Fifteen years ago, when I was living in Hong Kong, I was desperate to meet with David Beckham and his Real Madrid team mates who were visiting. I made my luck by contacting the Hong Kong Football Association and offering to translate for the visiting team for free. They accepted and as a result, I spent time socializing with David and the other football stars. Not one ounce of luck involved – well, apart from being lucky enough to have learned Spanish while working in South America!

Be optimistic and believe

Start telling yourself that you deserve good fortune. You need to believe it with every ounce of your body. It might sound crazy but studies do support this. How many negative people do you know whose lives are filled with luck and fortuitous moments? The conclusion to Richard Wiseman's ten-year study was that luck is a self-fulfilling prophecy and that so much of your good or bad fortune is a result of your mindset.

KEEP A CLOSE EYE ON YOUR BALANCE SHEET

'I'm always astonished to meet people who have no idea what they're worth.'

Imagine you're a company and your name is 'You Ltd' or 'You Inc.' What tasks would this involve? One of the most important is to keep track of your own financial performance, maintaining financial records and producing financial statements. A business normally creates three: a profit and loss statement, a cashflow statement and a balance sheet. Sales, expenses and profits are recorded in a profit and loss statement. This shows how profitable its range of business activities is. The cashflow statement records the inflows and outflows of cash. Both are important but it's even more important to know the details of your balance sheet.

The balance sheet lists all the things the business owns (called assets) and everything the business owes others (called liabilities). Added together these give a value of the business' net worth or how valuable the company is at that moment in time. Here's a simple example of a business with a net worth of $100,000.

Fixed assets		$000s	Fixed liabilities	$000s
	Properties	150	Property (mortgage) loans	120
	Machines	200	Other long-term loans	180
	Vehicles	50		
	IT equipment	40		
	Total fixed assets	440	Total fixed liabilities	300
Current assets		$000s	Current liabilities	$000s
	Cash in bank	10	Taxation (owing)	10
Customers (unpaid invoices)		20	Suppliers (unpaid invoices)	60
	Total current assets	30	Total current liabilities	70
Total assets (fixed + current)		470	Total liabilities (fixed + current)	370
Total net worth (also called total net assets) = total assets – total liabilities:			470 – 370	100

Note: 'Fixed' assets and liabilities are of a longer-term or permanent nature such as a house and mortgage. 'Current' refers to things receivable or payable in the short term such as a credit card bill.

44

Put it into action

Keep track of your net worth

Take a snapshot today of your total wealth, taking into account what you own (your assets) and the amounts you owe others (your liabilities). Try calculating this by creating your own personal balance sheet. You might make an Excel spreadsheet or use one of many online tools and apps. Once you've created it, you can easily keep it updated.

Your assets are those things of financial value to you. You should record the market values of assets such as your house, car and investments. Your liabilities will be things like a tax bill or bank mortgage.

You may struggle to remember all of your assets and liabilities so here's a list of the most common to check off against:

Your possible assets	Your possible liabilities
• House, land and other property	• House loan (mortgage)
• Cars, motorbike, boat	• Student loan
• Computer equipment	• Car loan
• Furniture, tools	• Loan from family or friends
• Financial products (e.g. shares, bonds, mutual funds)	• Bank overdraft
	• Payday loan
• Bank balance	• Tax bills due
• Pension	• Amount due to others such as a credit card
• The value of your business	bill

Have a goal for your future net worth

Once you know the current value of your net worth, set yourself a goal of how much you want to grow it and by when. Align this target with the broader financial goals you mapped out in Chapter 3.

KEEP YOUR INTEGRITY INTACT

'Success built on quicksand is worth nothing.'

At the end of 2018, the combined head of Nissan, Renault and Mitsubishi was fired. As one of the world's top business leaders, Carlos Ghosn had been incredibly successful in his role, earning millions over the last decade as he steered his car manufacturing group to success. His fall from grace was unexpected and based upon claims he had lied to the tax authorities about the size of his pay. He is one example of many people whose success was built on sand.

It is very easy and tempting to cut corners in pursuit of financial wealth. There are myriad ways people act without integrity:

- Faking sales figures, financial accruals and other numbers to ensure they earn their full year-end bonus, win a salary increase or job promotion.
- Selling a car and pretending that it is running smoothly when it isn't, or selling a house without disclosing the development plans next door, in order to sell assets quickly for the highest possible price.
- Claiming a particular qualification to get a better paid position.
- Lying to banks, investors, clients, suppliers or even family members to get a loan, sell dodgy products or delay paying for something.

Always keep your integrity intact. Never cut corners.

Remember all you have is your reputation.

45

Put it into action

Have your eyes wide open

Be observant and careful and don't allow yourself to get caught up in any form of deception. Always be on the lookout for potential lapses in integrity and ethics. This can take many forms, from someone offering you amazing investing tips that you suspect would constitute insider trading to your boss encouraging you to boost sales numbers artificially at year-end.

When you face situations like these, be ready to decline them and step away. When it warrants it, be ready to speak up and report it to the relevant authorities.

Guide others

Help keep other people honest by reminding and encouraging them to act with integrity.

IF IT AIN'T BROKE ...

'Every time I try tinkering with something that is working just fine, the darn thing stops working.'

Two experts in behavioural finance, Brad Barber and Terrance Odean, studied the performance of thousands of US day traders and found that those who traded the *most* made the *least*. In fact, the most active traders did at least 7% worse than the least active traders.

There are times when a tendency to tinker can be a strength, when a keenness to dabble or re-arrange is really useful. The danger is that if you automatically apply that tendency to your finances, it can lead to lower returns. If you were to take every piece of financial advice and act upon it, scared to miss out on the next financial opportunity, you'd be broke in a very short time.

Developing patience and a long-term view is the best guarantee of success, so that you don't feel compelled to jump at every 'great deal'.

Sometimes it's better just to leave well alone.

46

Put it into action

Be structured and systematic

You're investing for the long haul, so remember, in a lot of cases with money, 'set and forget' is the best course of action. Remember that more activity around your money doesn't necessarily mean more money.

If you've got plenty of excess cash, you can get away with chasing long shots, but assuming you're not so flush, it is wise to take a different approach.

- Explore how comfortable you are with your current investments. Understand the risks and returns involved with each and acknowledge the reasons why you're holding them.
- Decide which investments you really want to hold onto and which you could cash in, to free up the money for new and better opportunities.
- As and when you become aware of new opportunities, decide if they're of interest to you. If yes, do your homework and investigate the pros and cons.
- If it appears to be a good use of your funds, cash in one of your lower return or less important investments or use your existing cash or borrowings.

Sometimes you *do* need to fix what isn't broken

If you anticipate issues in the future around a particular investment, then adjusting your exposure makes good business sense. For example, the housing market might be stable now, but if you believe prices are about to fall, you may be right in selling up.

SECOND-HAND CARS ARE WISE INVESTMENTS

'Value – here one year and gone the next.'

Some assets lose their value very quickly, often in a way that's so uniform it can easily be predicted. Cars for example follow a very predictable pattern of declining re-sale value, and it's the same for phones, fridges, dishwashers, washing machines ...

	Car	Fridge
New purchase price	$10,000	$200
Price at end of Year 1	$8,000	$130
Price at end of Year 2	$6,000	$60
Price at end of Year 3	$4,000	$30
Price at end of Year 4	$2,000	$0

Of course it varies a little by brand and by country, but the underlying pattern is the same: sharp, predictable falls in re-sale value. Accountants refer to this as depreciation or amortization. The fall in value is meant to reflect wear and tear and cars and white goods are called high depreciation assets because they're subject to lots of it.

You don't need to be a genius to see that these aren't the sorts of things you should invest in or spend much money on if you want to maintain or grow your wealth.

47

Put it into action

Why pay a premium?

If you want something that you know will quickly fall in value, why would you buy it brand new? OK, so we all want the most up to date stuff sometimes, but it seems foolish to continually follow this approach with everything.

Invest in low depreciating assets

When it comes to investing your capital, steer clear of anything that's sure to fall in value. All investments rise and fall in value, for any number of reasons, but it's reckless to put your money into assets that will automatically lose value.

If cars or vinyl records are your thing, then purchase rare antique cars, or old records in mint condition. They keep their value and can even increase over time.

STAND TALL AND SMILE

'Just because you are not speaking does not mean that you are not communicating.'

Body language can be a powerful tool in helping you achieve financial success. Research by Harvard University's Amy Cuddy, published in *Psychological Science* in 2018, concluded that people adopting an expansive or power posture feel and act more powerful than those who don't. Basically, standing like Superman – tall, arms on your hips or away from your body – increases your sense of power.

In an earlier study also published in *Psychological Science*, two University of California Berkeley psychologists, Michael Kraus and Dacher Keltner, found that non-verbal body language reveals a person's socioeconomic status (SES). SES is determined by factors such as wealth, career and schools attended.

Use body language to your advantage, both in terms of how it can make you feel and the messages it sends to others. Stand upright, speak clearly, smile. Most of all, don't let your body language contradict you. Neuroscientists at Colgate University in New York State found that when non-verbal signs are not aligned with what you're saying, your verbal message is lost. In other words, people just don't hear what you're trying to communicate.

Act like Superman – and you can be Superman!

Put it into action

Create amazing first impressions

Research by Janine Willis and Alexander Todorov found that opinions formed within only a tenth of a second were highly correlated with opinions formed without any time constraint. In other words, in no time at all, we are able to decide how trustworthy, serious, ambitious, confident or tough another person is.

It doesn't matter who you need to impress, the first few seconds are key. Those in front of you – investors, bankers, staff, clients – will form an impression of you almost immediately. So:

- Prepare well. Be thoughtful about your clothes, shoes, hair and make-up.
- Always make eye contact and have a firm handshake. A University of Iowa study of job interviewees found that strong handshakes were always perceived more favourably than limp ones.
- Never slouch and don't fidget. CareerBuilder.com surveyed 2,500 hiring managers, and one third cited fidgeting by a candidate makes them less likely to be hired.

Read other people's body language

As you negotiate with bankers, business partners, investors and staff make sure you watch them well. Observe what they're not saying as much as what they are saying. If you can't read their body language, you risk missing half the conversation.

AVOID BEING LOCKED IN

'Wealth isn't about the amount of money you have. It's about the amount of choices and options available to you.'

For your money to grow, you normally pay the price of not having instant or cost-free access to it. That's the difference between liquid and illiquid investments.

- The most liquid investment is a bank or building society current account – very liquid but giving you a negligible interest rate.
- When investing in property you can only regain your money through selling, which takes time. If you need your money in a hurry, a quick sale might mean selling at a lower price than otherwise. You can of course obtain cash through re-mortgaging or renting out the property.
- You can get your money out of fixed-term deposits but you might be charged a fee, or worse, lose all the interest earned on the lifetime of the deposit.
- Getting money out of mutual funds or other investment vehicles can attract steep penalties if you can't stick to an agreed notice period.
- Some investments lock you in for years. An annuity is an illiquid savings scheme often sold along with a life insurance policy.

Being locked into an investment only becomes a problem when either you desperately need the money or the investment is falling in value and you want to cut your losses.

Always read the small print!

49

Put it into action

Know what you're getting into

Avoid getting unexpectedly trapped in an investment and being unable to move your money when you need to. Before signing anything, always check the small print.

When you create your personal balance sheet, add a notes section. For each of your financial assets and investments add a short summary of:

- how easily each fund, bank deposit or other investment can be liquidated and your funds returned to you. Note any notice periods, how notice must be given and to whom
- any penalties and fees incurred in redeeming or taking back early your money.

You are now ready and prepared for the day you need to urgently move your assets and investments.

Keep some cash

If much of your wealth is in a mixture of illiquid investments, be sure to keep sufficient in cash – not under your bed but in easy to access bank or building society accounts. Re-visit Chapter 19 to explore how much in readily available funds, if any, you choose to keep.

It's wise to sometimes 'lock in'

You might choose to lock some money into a long-term investment that you can't easily get your hands on, to ensure you don't spend or give it away too easily.

PASSIVE INCOME IS FREEDOM

'It's really cool when you can make money while sleeping!'

Let's just say for a moment you are no longer able to work. Where will your income come from? Can you visualize how you will survive financially? The wealthy don't have this worry. When they stop, their income keeps on flowing. They're not worried about missing work and not being paid, and the secret is passive income.

Passive income is often regular and recurring in nature but it may not be. It might also be varied in size and timing. Examples are anything you are able to earn with minimal or no effort:

- You renovate a house that you buy or inherit, giving it to a property management firm to rent out and manage the day to day issues with any tenants. You sit back and receive the rental income.
- You invest in a well-known and reputed mutual fund, simply receiving quarterly updates along with an annual profit (return), which you can leave in your account to be re-invested or take out as income – similar to compound interest on a deposit account.
- You run a business that serves clients through a subscription model. For example, clients pay an annual fee for membership of a health club where you are a silent/non-active shareholder, simply receiving annual dividend payments.

Passive income is income and capital growth that is generated continually, even while you're asleep!

50

Put it into action

Have a passive income plan

What will it take to create the passive income streams you need so that you create income flows that help you meet your life and financial goals without having to spend forever managing them?

Start with what interests you and what is available to you. You could:

- become a landlord renting out property through Airbnb
- invest in blue chip company shares and enjoy steady dividend streams
- leave funds with a stockbroker or fund manager, allowing them to move your money around to maximize your returns and capital growth
- invest in a few start-ups or SMEs (small- and medium-sized enterprises) as a silent investor. Passive income may not be assured but were it to come it could be large.

Aim to work only a couple of hours a week

Once you've determined how you will create passive income flows, you need to manage your time and determine how many hours you want to spend on growing and managing your passive income streams and how much you want to outsource to a stockbroker, accountant and/or fund manager. There are online tracking tools, investment sites and apps you can use to reduce and streamline your workload.

Don't spend your capital

Capital is the source of your passive income. Take great care to protect it. You may struggle to grow it, but be sure not to let it fall in value, either through spending it on non-income generating things or failing to cut your losses when it falls in value.

BE A PASSIONATE EXPERT

'Do what you love. Do it so well that others love you doing it.'

If you want to be rich, become an expert. Expertise enables you to maximize what you can earn in any given situation, whether you're working for others, self-employed or a full-time investor. Expert employees are more valuable, sought after and highly paid; expert business owners run better businesses; expert day traders and property developers make higher returns.

Achieving expertise takes determined practice. You have to spend time reading, learning, listening and doing. How long varies but it won't always take the 10,000 hours that's often quoted.

Becoming an expert is a journey and just as journeys are easier if you know where you are, when you're building expertise you need to know what level you're at, at any given moment – and to be realistic about your progress with yourself and others.

Pretending to know it all where money's involved is a sure way of losing it.

Put it into action

What is your expertise?

Bill Gates was an expert in early PC operating systems and has now become expert in global philanthropy and solving global health issues. JK Rowling is an expert in writing fiction. Where does your actual, or potential, expertise lie? Think of your technical skills but don't forget your soft skills, such as communication.

In your early years, gain expertise over money

In your twenties, building up experience, knowledge and understanding about money is most important, as these are the foundation of your future expertise and the basis for you creating value and wealth.

Enjoy becoming an expert

Expertise comes with time and practice. It's difficult to devote time to something you're not passionate about but it can be done. There are plenty of partners at law firms and accounting practices who don't enjoy law or accounting.

Take care in areas where you're not an expert

When you play in areas where you're not an expert, be prepared for sub-optimal outcomes. You might find you earn less than others in your field or organization, get lower returns on your investments, make less on your properties, or struggle to get your business off the ground.

And if all else fails, pay others for *their* expertise.

TURN YOUR BACK ON THE HERD

'Don't follow the crowd if the crowd is poor.'

It's hard to buck the trend. Humans like what psychologists refer to as social proof. We're more likely to do something if others have already done it. University of Pennsylvania psychologist Jonah Berger found in his experiments that participants were at least 10% more likely to buy something if they knew that others had already bought it, compared with situations where they were not told of other people's preferences.

One thing to bear in mind when it comes to money though: if the vast majority of people are doing something, it can pay to do the opposite. The *vast majority* of people aren't financially successful, but you are going to be.

Ultimately, if you are going to be a wise investor and creator of wealth, you will have to make up your own mind.

Sometimes you need to do what other people are doing; other times you need to go your own way.

52

Put it into action

Sense-check what you hear and see

There are some very convincing people around and it can be hard not to be taken in by strongly expressed ideas and opinions: 'What, you're holding no gold in your portfolio, in this market?', 'You mean you actually bought a property in the city? In this falling market!', 'You're still holding your shares in ABC plc? I sold mine last month and can sleep easy watching the company struggle.'

Hear and process any advice you're given, but also know your own reasoning, your own financial plans and your risk tolerances.

To be or not to be contrarian

Sometimes you need to follow the herd, sometimes you need to buck the trend. The difficulty is in knowing when. What would you do in these common scenarios?

- A company you own shares in is going bankrupt, its share price falling. The masses are selling their shareholdings. Do you follow the herd or buck the trend?
- A well-known and traditionally successful Fortune 500 group you own shares in is reporting very poor annual results. Its share price falls as many investors get out on the back of the reports. Do you follow the herd or buck the trend?

In both scenarios, you need to study the facts, take advice and make a decision that works for you. In the first example you may decide that it's unlikely the share price will recover anytime soon and you can't justify holding onto the shares. In this case, following the herd is the sensible option. On the other hand, in the second example you may decide from your analysis that the share price and company performance will come back to their long-term trends and moving averages, despite the current dip. In that case bucking the trend is the right decision for you – holding your shares and perhaps even buying more to take advantage of the situation.

Gaining the wisdom to know how to act involves a combination of learning, trial and error, and, perhaps most importantly, taking excellent advice.

EXCELLENT ADVICE COMES AT A PRICE

'If you think an expert is expensive to hire, try finding the money to clean up after an amateur.'

If you break a leg, do you stay in bed and google home remedies or do you find a doctor? Reading medical websites is definitely the easier option, but how effective is it? It's the same with financial advice. With a simple issue you might just google: 'which high street bank has the best savings account interest?' or 'which online share trading platforms are most popular?' or 'what are the rental yields on apartments where I live?'

When you're facing larger money issues, you need more professional and accurate advice. What if you need to:

- understand the tax implications of various investment options facing you?
- assess your risk tolerance?
- know the range of financial options open to you?
- explore the pros and cons of taking money early from your pension scheme?
- complete your tax return or company's financial accounts?
- decide how to hold your wealth – in your name, in a company or in trust?

There is no comprehensive and free health service equivalent in the wealth creation business. You just have to be ready to pay for help. In the past it might have been questionable but governments do a good job regulating financial advice these days, with accreditation bodies such as the CFP in the US and rules to reduce the risks of being cheated.

Are you ready to pay for advice?

53

Put it into action

Start now

Paying out small amounts on fees can be money well spent, particularly if you've been building up your wealth to date without any formal advice.

- Review your financial situation with an advisor at your high street bank.
- Learn about available forms of additional advice at websites such as (UK) www.moneyadvice-service.org.uk or (US) www.wisebread.com and www.bankingsense.com
- Review options for optimizing your house financing with a mortgage advisor.
- Have a local accountant help you review or complete your annual tax return.

Move onto bigger things

As you build up your wealth, consider getting good quality advice on topics such as:

- opening an offshore bank account
- moving your wealth into a trust – onshore or offshore – to legally minimize tax obligations and to make inheritance smoother
- getting regular professional financial markets advice from a private bank or a stockbroking firm.

Reach out and speak to people. Today you might be viewed as being too small to be taken on as a client by certain private banks and stockbroking firms if they have minimum investment thresholds, but if you persist you can find really good advice and help, even if it's a one-off.

Set up a family office

A family office is a dedicated professional team hired to manage your wealth. You may not be ready for that now but as soon as you have built up enough wealth and can justify the expense, set one up. In late 2018, *The Economist* reported in an article entitled 'How the super-rich invest' that: '*Largely unnoticed, family offices have become a force in investing, with up to $4 trillion of assets—more than hedge funds and equivalent to 6% of the value of the world's stock markets*.'

THERE IS A TIME AND PLACE

'It is essential to understand where you are in your journey of life and to financially plan and act appropriately.'

These are the six stages our lives typically go through (adapt to fit your own situation!):

1. You depend on family to support you through school, college or university.
2. You start your first job, making ends meet but struggling to save.
3. You begin to create wealth through owning your first property and sharing your life with a partner.
4. You have children, investing in their education while growing your career and wealth.
5. You become an empty nester, enjoying the last few years of working life and having inheritance windfalls as parents pass away.
6. You retire, looking after your health and living off your pension and investment incomes.

What financial stage are you in? It's important to know where you are today so that you can understand your current financial situation and be mindful of the later phases still to come. If you're in your twenties or thirties, it can be very hard to imagine yourself in the empty nester or retired phases, but you'll get there.

During each of these phases your financial inflows, outflows and net wealth will vary considerably from one period to another. It's important to appreciate this and to factor it in to your financial planning, actions and goal setting.

> During each phase of your life, protect and grow your wealth as much as possible.

54

Put it into action

Maximize your net worth at each stage

Here are some things to consider at the different life stages:

- As a student, be thoughtful about how employable you will be when choosing courses and where you study. Try to keep student loans to a minimum, and take on weekend or holiday jobs. Find work experience that helps make you more employable.
- When starting out in your career, try to avoid splurging on material things, or overpaying on rent. Automatically save part of your salary each month and retain your 'student mentality' of always looking for great deals. Travel and enjoy life, but do it cost effectively.
- As your salary grows, decide whether to pay off any loans (student, mortgage, car, credit card etc.) faster than the minimum or default rate. Consider setting aside more to put into your pension scheme on top of what your employer takes out. In the US, maximize your 401(k) contributions to give you more savings in the future.
- With your partner, decide whether to merge your finances or keep them separate. Consciously plan to optimize your joint tax liabilities.
- If you have children, give them savings accounts and ensure you claim any government benefits such as the UK's child allowance. Teach your children about money, saving and finance in general.
- Once you become an empty nester, you'll need to make decisions about whether to maintain your family home or downsize and use the surplus cash to create more passive income.
- Consider whether you can pay off all your borrowings, including mortgages on investment properties, before you retire.

SHORT-TERM PAIN FOR LONG-TERM GAIN

'Sacrificing £1 today will give you £2 tomorrow.'

You won't build up future wealth by giving yourself an easy time today. There's a very common misconception that it's better to borrow as much as you can now, to get as big a mortgage as you can, and to push the payment terms as far into the future as possible. But do you really want to give your future self the ongoing challenge of repaying what you borrowed today?

Let's imagine you and your partner want to buy a house costing $500,000. You have $50,000 saved up for a deposit, another $50,000 held in various financial investments, and enough set aside to pay all the legal fees and other costs. On your current combined salaries, you could afford monthly mortgage repayments of up to about $3,000 but $2,000 per month would be more comfortable and wouldn't curtail your lifestyle. Assume a fixed mortgage interest rate of 4%.

Which mortgage and repayment schedule seems most appropriate?

Option	Amount borrowed	Own money invested	Years to repay	Monthly repayment	Total interest paid
A	$450,000	$50,000	30	$2,148	$323,413
B	$400,000	$100,000	30	$1,910	$287,578
C	$450,000	$50,000	20	$2,727	$204,459
D	$400,000	$100,000	20	$2,424	$181,741
E	$450,000	$50,000	15	$3,329	$149,147
F	$400,000	$100,000	15	$2,959	$132,575

There are some big decisions to make here around how much to borrow, how long for and how far to stretch your monthly repayments. To help answer the question, try to give it some context: in 30 years' time, will you thank yourself for the decisions you make today?

You have to make sacrifices today for your future wealth.

55

Put it into action

Decide how much short-term pain you can endure

In this example, think about the following:

- How important is it to maintain your monthly disposable income so that you can keep up the same lifestyle? Could you forgo spending today to more speedily pay off your mortgage? Is it likely that you or your partner will gain job promotions and salary increases over the next couple of years, making future monthly repayments easier than today?
- How good are the returns on the £50,000 in other investments? If you use it for the house purchase, what returns do you lose? If you invest all of your available £100,000, how do you cope on a 'rainy day', when you need the funds?
- Having 30 years rather than 15 or 20 to repay the loan makes a big difference in terms of total interest paid, as well as giving you differing monthly repayment amounts. If you visualize it, do you feel better paying off the loan earlier or waiting the full 30 years? Bear in mind that depending on your age, you might have retired before paying it all off.

Understand the benefits of paying off your mortgage faster

It's important to consider all the benefits of paying off your mortgage over a shorter term:

- You own the property outright sooner. The entire value of the property becomes your asset.
- You will have repaid more of the principal by the time you choose to sell and upgrade. This is one of the key reasons never to sign up to interest-only repayment mortgages. No matter how appealing they may seem in the first few years, the principal will not have fallen because all your money is going on interest payments.
- Paying more interest each month gives you the extra tax benefit of being able to offset interest payments against your income.
- If house prices fall, you will hopefully have less of a negative equity issue than if you were repaying your mortgage more slowly. In other words you'll be less likely to sell for a price that's less than the amount you still owe the bank.
- If you faced financial struggles in the future, you could re-mortgage and seek extended payment terms.

BE EDUCATED NOT ENTERTAINED

'Wealthy people have one TV and many books. Poor people have many TVs and no space for books.'

Do you spend your evenings watching TV or reading? How many non-fiction books, journals and magazines do you read in a month? It's never been studied but I'd bet there's a correlation between reading and becoming wealthy. Every billionaire I've ever known stresses the importance of learning and reading in their success.

- Li Ki-Shing has spoken about knowledge determining your fate. He should know; born into poverty, he has become one of the world's richest individuals.
- Bill Gates said that '*reading fuels a sense of curiosity about the world, which I think helped drive me forward in my career and in the work that I do now with my foundation*'.
- Richard Branson advises: 'Read *what others have done, take what works for you and adapt it into your own life*.'

But as well as informal lifelong learning, should you go back to formal education to help you become richer? Studies do show that university graduates earn more than school leavers. In the US, a 2014 Pew Research Center study concluded that the '*median yearly income gap between high school and college graduates is around $17,500* [per annum]'. A UK Department for Education study concluded that '*in 2016, working age (aged 16–64) graduates earned on average £9,500 more than non-graduates* [per annum], *while postgraduates earned on average £6,000 more than graduates* [per annum]'.

This extra average salary might appeal to you, but it does vary widely by degree subject and the additional income doesn't, on its own, guarantee that you'll achieve financial freedom.

Perhaps the final word here is the fact that many of today's super-rich left school at 16 or 18 while others quit university before graduating!

Changing habits is not easy but is an effort that will pay off handsomely.

56

Put it into action

Hone your learning habits

It can take a couple of years to make it a habit, but reading and learning for at least 30 minutes a day will pay you back handsomely as you take on new ideas and learn new techniques. Browse business magazines and newspapers like *Inc.*, *Investors Chronicle*, *Harvard Business Review*, *The Economist*, *Monocle*, *Time*, *Strategy Plus* and the *Financial Times*. Reading newspapers from all over the world – you'll be amazed at the new and unexpected insights and business ideas that come to you.

Build your informal learning

Try the following as starting points for building your informal learning:

- Read biographies of entrepreneurs.
- Get used to reading companies' annual returns to help you choose which shares to buy.
- Find books on innovation, design thinking and creativity to help you grow your business.
- Read self-help books to find ways of boosting your communication skills, self-esteem or selling skills.

Your mental workout regime

Find the time to read, learn and study by implementing a '30 minutes a day' mental exercise rule. Do whatever you need to do to make it work for you; use a Kindle or an iPad, or listen to audio books on your daily commute. Skim read or speed read. Do whatever it takes to be a life-long learner, unlearning and re-learning as you go.

DO NOT BE SWAYED BY DOOM AND GLOOM

'When someone dies in a car accident, do you sell your cars and never drive again?'

Each week we read all kinds of headlines:

'Stocks Fall, Wiping Out Gains for the Year'

'Oil Price Collapse Is Sending Shockwaves Through Global Markets'

'UK on the Verge of Brexit-induced Economic Collapse'

'Eurozone Risks Imploding Under Weight of Ballooning Debt'

The media loves a scary headline and nothing sells better than fear, worry, anxiety and negativity. Very little is more exciting to newspaper editors and TV presenters than graphs of falling stock market indices, currencies and property prices. I'm surprised we're not all keeping our wealth under the bed or in gold bars. Well, it makes great copy and sells a few newspapers.

You have to know what's going on, but not blindly believe everything you hear. It's important not to automatically react to stories in the news in an attempt to protect your investments. When the media reports talk about the end of diesel vehicles, it doesn't mean you have to rush to sell your automotive industry shares and bonds. Instead look for the truth.

> Understand the facts and fundamentals of the financial products and businesses you are investing in beyond the shock headlines.

57

Put it into action

Know the fundamentals

Base your investment decisions on an analysis of the fundamentals of assets you are investing in. Get a sense for the soundness of an asset, its price and prospects. For any company you're considering holding shares or bonds in, the fundamentals include:

- How stable is the revenue base?
- How much competition is there?
- Are raw material costs and supplies an issue?
- How large are the profit margins?
- What is the product pipeline and size of R&D and investments?
- What is the size, type and maturity of any debt held by the company?
- How is the company's cashflow, including the regularity and size of any dividend payments and share buybacks?
- To what degree is the company's business recession proof?

Your ability to understand a company's fundamentals is greatly enhanced by learning about financial statements and financial ratios, something we'll come to.

For a market index (such as Nasdaq or the FTSE100), individual shares, Forex or other tradeable assets, you need to understand the charts showing historical price movements as well as the volume of shares being bought and sold, to show if any price movements are likely to be sustained.

Be wary of wildly positive news

The same logic applies when the media and financial analysts are talking up some asset class, product or index. Just as you would do with falling stocks, pause and look at the fundamentals. If in doubt, seek and pay for expert advice and opinion. Analysing charts and fundamentals is really quite tedious for most people and very time consuming. Fund managers are paid to do it, so consider leaving money with them and focusing on other types of assets such as property.

INVEST IN THINGS YOU ENJOY

'Only invest in things you would be happy to hold and use in the event that the market for them closes.'

You can't succeed when your work drives you nuts. No one consistently excels at tasks they don't enjoy. You make mistakes, get bored, neglect details and lack the energy for being creative and innovative. There isn't a single multi-millionaire or billionaire who made their wealth through activities they hated.

But whatever you're into, there are motivating and interesting ways of making money. You just have to find what works for you and make the money a byproduct. For me that means:

- renovating old properties to rent or sell
- writing books to inspire others, bringing me regular royalty income and speaking engagement fees
- building up my coaching and training business.

Even within these passions, I still have preferences. I only buy properties I could imagine wanting to live in – and I sometimes do – I only write books on topics that interest me, and I only coach and mentor clients I really enjoy working with.

What do you enjoy doing that could make money as a byproduct?

58

Put it into action

Trial and error

It's very hard to know if you're going to enjoy something before you've actually done it. You can guess or have a gut feel, get excited by other people's enthusiasm, but it's only when you try something that you can actually see how energized, motivated, interested and passionate it makes you.

Even then, you might need some time to arrive at a balanced opinion. Initially you might just be sold on the novelty of it and enjoy the sense of doing something new. On the other hand, as a novice you might be overwhelmed and walk away from something too soon.

Enjoyment helps you through downturns

Enjoying what you spend your time and money on will see you through the hard times when markets are falling and you can't offload or sell something. Think how much better it is to be stuck with assets, investments and property you like having, rather than those you hate.

Be open to not enjoying your work

Remember, your greatest financial opportunities might not always be in assets and tasks that appeal to you. Sometimes it does just come down to getting money in the bank. Be prepared to get your hands dirty from time to time so that you can focus most on what you love, whether that's property, start-ups, derivatives, put options ... whatever floats your boat.

WORK SMART

'You can always buy more money, but you can never buy more time.'

Burning out is a great way to make sure you never get the chance to enjoy your money or your time. And if you're working 52 weeks a year and putting in 18-hour days, you will burn out.

Look out for the tell-tale signs of overcommitment. Are you getting up at 5 am and packing every day with actions until you fall asleep at night, chasing multiple goals and driving yourself to complete an unrealistic weekly to-do list? We all do this every now and again but if it becomes the norm, it's time to put on the brakes.

Make time to pause, re-charge, reflect and explore. Look at how the world's richest people find a balance, from Richard Branson starting his mornings on Necker Island walking and reading, through to Jerry Seinfeld making time each day to meditate.

Your financial goals are there to direct and focus you but you should never become a slave to them. You're going to have to work harder than average, as you already know, but you need to work smarter than average too. You need to learn to make comfortable and sustainable choices about how you use your time, allowing you to get the important things done without killing yourself.

> True wealth is not measured in financial terms but in having time.

59

Put it into action

Be brutal

Be smart with your time, whether you're an employee, investor and/or entrepreneur. Observe how your time is used and compare that to how you *need* to use it.

Identify activities that serve you and those you can shorten or eliminate

Monitor your day and do anything necessary to streamline it:

- Are there any trivial and unimportant distractions that you could stop yourself being drawn into?
- What activities could be eliminated or shortened?
- Are you tied up in too many meetings? Are there any you could skip or attend only the parts that are relevant to you?

Automate, outsource and delegate

Making money often means being involved in multiple activities, from holding down a day job to investing time and money in other businesses. Time pressure can build up, so identify any tasks that could be easily, and cost effectively, changed, automated or given to others to do:

- Pay an accountant to do your book-keeping.
- Hire a property manager.
- Switch to automated banking services.

Build a team

You can't do everything alone. Later on in the book, we'll look at how hiring staff could help you achieve your financial dreams.

ARE YOU LISTENING?

'I have never known any truly successful person who wasn't also a great listener.'

It always makes me laugh when someone says 'I hear you'. Hearing what someone is saying is completely different to listening to them. When you listen, you take information in, process it, learn, and apply it to your decision making.

Being a good listener is essential to building wealth because the consequences of *not* listening can be disastrous to your finances, whether it's failing to follow the guidance of your financial advisor and investing in the wrong products, misunderstanding a key customer's concerns and losing them as a client or failing to hear a tenant's requests meaning they give early notice on their tenancy.

It's easy to fool yourself into thinking you're good at listening. In a 2015 global study by Accenture, 96% of those surveyed said they were good listeners, but they also admitted to being distracted and multitasking. Don't be fooled. Another study at the University of Minnesota by Ralph Nichols and Leonard Stevens shows the real picture. It concluded that *'immediately after the average person has listened to someone talk, he remembers only about half of what he has heard—no matter how carefully he thought he was listening'*.

Listening is hard. Your mind is always racing, your focus is constantly shifting between the past and the future, and like everyone else, you are filled with anxieties and worries. Fortunately, active listening skills are easy to learn and perfect.

Be a better – and wealthier – person: learn to listen!

Put it into action

Practise active listening

You owe it to yourself and everyone you interact with to ensure you listen well. *They* will feel valued and respected, and *you* will be better informed.

- Be present. Sit or stand still when listening to others. Put your phone away and look at the other person's face as they speak. Close your eyes as you listen to them on the phone. Look at the computer screen as you listen to them on a video conference.
- Show that you are listening. Nod, show agreement, say 'I follow', 'I understand'. Do not interrupt them.
- As someone is speaking, stop planning in your head what you want to say in response and just hear the other person.
- After they've spoken, pause and take on board what they've said.
- Before giving answers or justifications, discuss and agree that you're both on the same page.
- Show them (and yourself) that you understood what they were saying. Summarize back to them what you heard them say.
- Ask clarifying questions to make sure what you think you heard is actually what the other person was saying. This is very important when emotions are involved and someone's words may not be 100% clear and objective.
- Immediately make written notes of what was discussed. Email the other person a summary to make doubly sure you listened well.

NO CHEATING ON YOUR TAXES

'Taxation is the price you pay to live in a modern society.'

We're going to have to talk about tax at some point. It's not the most popular topic. Let's face it, no one loves paying it, many people love avoiding it.

There will always be plenty of advisors on hand to help save you a bit of money here and there. On one level that can seem like a nice way of building up your assets but you won't be truly wealthy without the peace of mind of knowing that you're on the right side of the law and contributing to society.

And if you need any more incentive, just think of the people who get caught out. Every year dozens of millionaires are accused of tax avoidance and often end up paying fines, legal costs and back taxes. Not to mention the reputational hit and future income generation prospects.

It's not always black and white. Sometimes you may not even know you're cheating. You might innocently think you're using a legal method of minimizing personal or corporate tax.

No one gets rich avoiding taxes – so don't be a mug.

Put it into action

Pay your fair share

There are many ways of minimizing your tax bills: shell companies, offshores, trusts, treating income differently, certain offsets, loopholes. There's an endless list of possibilities. The savings possibilities are huge. Bloomberg reported that in 2016 alone Google legally saved $3.7 billion in taxes through using shell companies in places like Ireland, the Netherlands and Bermuda. The rich pay large fees to their advisors to help them stay within the law while minimizing tax exposure. You can do the same. No one is asking you to over-pay.

At the same time, be careful of loopholes which, although technically legal, are unethical. Sure, you could get away with it, but you know it's wrong. Live with the right values and moral compass, so that you're happy paying your fair share - taking advantage of permitted allowances and deductions but steering clear of any dubious schemes.

Maximize tax-free saving schemes

Find out about the tax-free saving schemes the government runs where you live. Many countries have them. In the UK, you can invest in an Individual Savings Accounts (ISA) up to a certain limit each year and the savings earn interest tax-free. The allowance for the 2018/19 tax year was £20,000 and you could invest this in any combination of ISAs, for example £7,000 in a cash ISA, £3,000 in an innovative finance ISA and £10,000 in a stocks and shares ISA.

Report accurately

As you build up your assets and income flows, it's time to get someone else to complete your annual tax return for you and make sure you both agree on all your income sources and related expenses. Don't naively allow the accountant to under-report your income or incorrectly claim an allowance, thinking they're doing you a favour. They're not.

KNOW WHEN TO QUIT YOUR DAY JOB

'Work on your own goals and dreams. Or let other people pay you to work on theirs.'

Most of today's wealthy people were once paid employees, the majority of them moving on to own businesses, or to manage and grow their various investments. There are exceptions. You can become a multi-millionaire in some jobs but typically only in certain professions like law, accounting, investment banking, stockbrokers and traders, tech start-ups, surgeons, architects, to name just a few. In the US, according to a 2018 survey by the US Census, the median annual income for all employees was US$61,000, and for 25-year-olds it was US$34,000. The Office for National Statistics in the UK in 2017 calculated that the average annual salary across the UK was £27,271.

Walking away from a secure or dream job might be your springboard to fulfilling your financial dreams. There are amazing stories and inspiration everywhere you look. Take Emma Gannon who gave up her dream job in London with the publishing group Condé Nast to pursue her own business ideas, which now include the popular 'Ctrl Alt Delete' podcasts and a couple of best-selling books. Or Rick Wetzel and Bill Phelps who quit working for Nestlé to create the Wetzel's Pretzels food chain in the US.

Search out stories of people who've taken the plunge and walked away from secure jobs in pursuit of something. It's truly inspiring to see how people have gone about creating wealth and fulfilment just from an idea or a passion.

Will you stay on working as an employee indefinitely, set an end date, or make the leap to becoming your own boss now?

Your challenge is to know what's the right thing for *you*.

62

Put it into action

Know what drives you

If you are considering moving on from your day job, consider your motivations. Are you trying to escape from something, or is this genuinely an opportunity to increase your wealth and do something you really want to do?

Make preparations

Don't just ditch the day job without a plan. Prepare to leave while you're still working. And if you possibly can, prepare to the point where your side hustle is already earning you money and ready to become your main hustle. Use your safe time as an employee to:

• gain the skills you need
• study in the evenings or become accredited with a professional association or body
• network and make contacts so you can learn from the right people
• consider starting other ventures in your spare time.

Never a perfect moment

Don't procrastinate and delay quitting. Seek mentors and other people to give you advice, encouragement and support.

Make sure you're suited to being self-employed

It's OK to stay employed in the mainstream. Not everyone is suited to the uncertainties, risks, stress and responsibilities of being self-employed or simply managing money. Think long and hard before you quit your day job and if deep down you've realized that you prefer being an employee then this is the time to accept it.

WATCH OUT FOR 'LIFESTYLE CREEP'

'Never buy anything just to show off. Nobody cares.'

Bill Gates recalled in a Bloomberg interview that in the late 1970s he bought himself his first car, a Porsche 911, with his first cash windfall from owning Microsoft. So what do you do when your wealth starts rising? Do you upgrade your life, buy the latest sportscar, a bigger home, club memberships, exotic holidays, tailor-made clothes or move your kids to elite private schools? You worked for it, right, you deserve to enjoy it.

No one is stopping you enjoying your new-found wealth but if you already own a car, why change it just because your salary rises? If you love your home, why upgrade to a more affluent neighbourhood when your investment income goes up? The danger comes when you automatically want to upgrade and have the best of everything. It's known as lifestyle creep and it's when you raise your expenditures and commitments to match your increased salary. It's the reason why far too many lottery winners lose all of their wealth within a few years.

Your lifestyle and spending choices shouldn't reflect your wealth and desire to impress others, they should reflect your own needs and values. Be like Warren Buffett. He reportedly still lives in the same house he bought for $31,500 in 1958 and drives a 2014 Cadillac XTS.

> Don't fall into the trap of spending to mask your insecurities and low self-esteem.

63

Put it into action

As your income rises, the percentage you spend should fall

It might sound too perfect, but as your salary rises, *save* the extra income. Don't spend any of it. For example, you earn $2,800 after tax each month. You get an 8% increase to $3,024. Instead of rolling the extra $224 into your monthly expenditure, set up or adjust an autopay to transfer it automatically into your saving account, ideally on the same day you're paid. Hopefully, you were already saving some of your previous salary and the $224 is additional savings.

If you don't, you'll happily spend every single bit of the extra $224. It's not that much per month, is it, except when you realize that over 12 months, it would leave you with an extra $2,688 and after two years $5,376. Now it's starting to add up nicely. This would contribute towards the deposit on your first property purchase.

Similarly, when you earn an unexpected one-off amount of money from an annual bonus, inheritance or unplanned dividends payments – save or invest the entire amount.

The rich don't always buy 'haute couture'

A good habit to get into is to write a shopping list before you head out. Pause before thinking about buying anything that's not on the list and only buy what you need. Heed the advice of Warren Buffett: *'If you buy things you don't need, you will soon sell things you need.'*

No need to be an early adopter

Minimize those 'I must be the first to buy the new iPhone model' purchases. Often these are simply ego or insecurity purchases, and not things you need in your life.

UNDERSTAND NUMBERS

'We are becoming a society of financially illiterate people.'

Sorry to drop it on you, but if you want to grow your wealth you need to become financially literate. That means being ready to understand the various aspects of the world of investing, accounting and finance. You need to have the skills and knowledge to:

- make informed and accurate decisions relating to your finances
- understand what is happening to your money and investments
- be able to compare options open to you
- appreciate the reasons and impacts of movements in assets, prices and markets
- be comfortable with the risks and range of possible outcomes.

I was fortunate in already being a qualified accountant and ex-CFO when I started to focus on building my wealth. You don't need to become a qualified accountant, tax expert or chartered financial analyst but at a minimum, I encourage you to pay close attention to the areas covered in this chapter. Even if you intend to outsource much of your financial decision making to others like stockbrokers and fund managers, understanding the basics will help you keep a close eye on the decisions and actions financial advisors and accountants are making on your behalf and enable you to talk with them in financial detail.

It's time to educate yourself – are you ready?

64

Put it into action

Go back to school

Take online courses, read books and attend evening classes. You could choose topics such as: Finance for Non-Financial Managers, Personal Finance Mastery, Understanding Investing and Trading. Ask experts to teach you and learn by doing (being careful not to lose any of your wealth in the process). There are numerous excellent websites with fantastic explanations and glossaries, such as www.investopedia.com. Start reading the *Financial Times*, *Investors Chronicle* and *The Economist*. And start looking at the tables showing the prices and price movements in the markets you're investing in.

As a minimum, learn about and understand:

- *Balance sheets*: for more on this see Chapter 44.
- *Profit and loss statements*: remember that a profit or a loss is the difference between all sales and income revenue minus all the expenses and overheads. There are many definitions for a profit, such as EBITDA and operating profit. They are either before or after tax, interest, depreciation etc.
- *Financial ratios*: there are a number which you need to know, including gross or net sales margin, and return on capital employed.
- *Compound interest*: for more on this see Chapter 28.
- *The net present value (NPV) of money*: $100 earned today and $100 gained in a year's time do not have the same value today. The $100 that you earn in the future, in today's value, is worth less than $100 by a factor of the interest rate your money could earn. For example, $95.24 earning interest at 5% per annum is worth $100 in one year's time.
- *Exchange rates*: for more on this see Chapter 34.
- *Investment terminology*: before investing in shares, bonds, derivatives, indices, funds etc., understand what they are. Learn how and why they move and what terminology is used in their markets, such as return on investment, earnings per share, price/earnings ratio, spread, bid price, market values, forward contract, put options and liquidity.
- *Percentage movements of assets*: for more on this see Chapter 80.

BUILD UP YOUR OPTIMISM

'The glass is always half full.'

An American psychologist, Barbara Fredrickson, has studied the impact of being positive and optimistic and the conclusions of her well-known work, known as the Broaden and Build theory, showed that:

- optimism and positivity improve your ability to solve problems and focus. They broaden the capacity of your brain
- pessimism on the other hand reduces your brain's ability to perform and to be creative because it reduces the functioning of your prefrontal cortex.

You will find it hard to achieve challenging financial goals if you're feeling and acting negative and down. Pessimism stops you working with passion and enthusiasm and reduces your ability to inspire and motivate those you're working with. This was clearly demonstrated in a study of newly recruited insurance sales teams by renowned positive psychologist Martin Seligman. He found that optimistic insurance salespeople sold 37% more policies than their pessimistic colleagues, with the pessimists wasting their energy on things that weren't going right.

Are you ready to build up your levels of optimism and positive thinking?

Put it into action

Focus on outcomes, not problems

Gabriele Oettingen, an NYU psychology professor, defines optimism as the expectations and judgement that you can do certain things in the future. That's what you have to focus on, giving your attention to the outcomes that you can and will achieve. One thing that can help in this process is acknowledging what you have achieved to date. Start writing a journal that combines your to-do lists with lists of what you've achieved.

Unlike Seligman's pessimistic insurance salespeople, avoid focusing on what's going wrong. Be aware of such details but don't dwell on them.

Avoid negative people

It helps if you can steer clear of pessimists. We all know someone who will give you 101 reasons why something can't be done. Walk away. Life is too short to waste one minute putting up with excessive negativity.

Be wary of over-optimism

Balance your optimism with realism. Some leaders and entrepreneurs are so positive they become blindly optimistic, totally convinced of what will happen. This can certainly help you steamroll obstacles and doubters but it can also cut you off from reality. Always listen to others and try to see what is really happening.

SEEK VALUE

'Why would you buy something at list price when you can get it at half price in a sale?'

Value investing is a very simple and powerful approach. The idea is that if you know the true value of something, you can save a lot of money only buying it when it's below that value, whether it's on sale, at auction, in a distressed sale or undervalued for any other reason.

Investors refer to this true value as intrinsic value and they always aim to buy assets that are trading at significant discounts to their intrinsic values. Value investing originated from stock markets investment and was made famous by Benjamin Graham, author of *The Intelligent Investor*, a bible to many investors over the last six decades.

In the simple example below, you can see the market prices are less than the intrinsic values. In all three cases this difference, called the discount or potential upside, is $60, but the difference in percentage terms varies. Holding a range of undervalued stocks is viewed as a high-return, low-risk portfolio.

Shares	Share's intrinsic value	Current market price of the share	Discount or potential upside (as % of current price)
A	$100	$40	$60 (150%)
B	$120	$60	$60 (100%)
C	$150	$90	$60 (67%)

Estimating a stock's intrinsic value isn't easy though. It involves looking at many variables, starting with the price/earnings ratio and the company's underlying financial performance, then comparing these to industry and stock market averages. Stock markets are populated by thousands of professional investors backed by financial institutions' models, analysis and high-speed share trading platforms. It's not easy to compete against them, but as an individual share trader, you can 'swim with them', looking for undervalued stocks, just as they do. If you aren't confident doing this, place your money with fund managers and leave their teams to do the hunting for you.

Why would you ever want to buy something that costs more than its intrinsic value?

Put it into action

Apply value investing principles to all of your wealth creation

You may not have the time and expertise to find undervalued stocks and other financial markets products, but you can apply the idea of only buying assets that are below their market price in other areas.

- *Day-trading*: if you do decide to manage your own share portfolio, be ready to invest time in research, focusing on stock markets and companies that you know well, or can get to know well. For example, I know of a retired executive from a large drugs company in London, who only invests in large pharmaceutical company shares. By focusing on an industry he knows well, he's able to find underpriced shares.
- *Property*: buying property at a discount to its market price is becoming a common way of making money. Property like this can be flipped (sold) 'as is', without any changes made, as soon as the market price rises. Alternatively, renovating a property before selling is an example of creating value. It's very common to increase a house's value by adding rooms, turning attics into bedrooms, creating basements and conservatories. According to a Zopa 2017 survey of renovations carried out in the UK, the average return on the cost of any renovations was 50%. The average profit per renovation project was £8,000.
- *Other asset classes*: this same logic applied to finding undervalued stocks and houses can be applied to all types of assets, including gold, artwork, vehicles and buying businesses.

START YOUR OWN BUSINESS

'Sometimes the only way to achieve your dreams is to become an entrepreneur.'

Most millionaires are self-employed and in a world where working for yourself and building a business from scratch is seen as the ultimate in self-actualization, it's no surprise that many of us are doing it. The growth rates are staggering. 42 million Americans were self-employed in 2018 according to MBO Partners, making up about 25% of the total US work force. In the UK, there are over 600,000 new start-ups each year according to data from the Centre for Entrepreneurs. Many are run by the owners and have no staff. In 2018 there were 4.3 million such so-called self-employed businesses. They made up 75% of all businesses in the UK, according to 2018 government data.

Financial success for entrepreneurs isn't assured, and relatively few companies achieve high levels of growth and multi-million sales. Most sole proprietors, if they're lucky, make the same as they would working for a salary, and start-up failure rates are high. In a study by Statistic Brain, the failure rate after five years of US companies is over 50%, and over 70% after ten years.

On the positive side, being your own boss gives you incredible freedom to be yourself and to choose what you create, with whom you work, which clients you serve and how much money you want to make. With these freedoms come the responsibility and stress of having to manage your own time, money and resources. And the fact that no one automatically pays you a salary each month.

> Being the master of your destiny as your own boss has so many benefits which outweigh the costs.

Put it into action

Love what you do

Only start a business in a product or service you love and will enjoy.

Have a business plan

Know how you are going to create value. Be able to articulate what you are producing, buying and selling, to whom, and at what price. Create a business plan, including financial forecasts and understanding your cashflow.

Set up the ideal legal entity

Take advice from an accountant or company secretary to help determine the ideal legal entity you need to create. Are you planning to remain as a one-person business or set up a company where you are only liable for the amount of capital you invest? Every country has a number of options, offering different taxation obligations.

Choose business partners carefully

Try to keep 100% of your company's ownership, only giving up a share if you really need a working business partner and/or investment partners (who may only provide money as capital, but not be involved in helping run the business).

Seek government support

Governments provide all kinds of support to new start-ups. In the US help is provided by various bodies, including the Small Business Administration. In the UK there have been a number of initiatives in recent years such as the Start Up Loans scheme and the Seed Enterprise Investment Scheme.

EMBRACE TECHNOLOGY

'The future is digital and technical. Make sure you're part of it.'

At the end of 2018, the world's six largest companies by market value were all in the technology and internet space: Apple, Amazon, Alphabet, Microsoft, Facebook and Alibaba. Bad news for the Luddites among you, you can't ignore technology in your pursuit of wealth.

The internet and related technologies have transformed and will continue to transform all aspects of modern life:

- Smartphones, emails, messaging and social media platforms have taken over as our communication channels.
- Money flows, business and financial transactions happen in seconds, with block chain and cryptocurrencies transforming old forms of contracting and payments.
- Websites and apps are where we buy, sell, learn, check and find everything, from ordering groceries to finding true love.
- Internet-enabled technologies are in our offices, factories, homes, cars and soon within our bodies.
- Robotics and AI are transforming all types of industries from manufacturing to services, including the health, education and government sectors.

Over half the world's population, or 4.2 billion people, were using the internet by 2018 according to Internet World Stats, and together we spent a combined one billion years online according to an estimate by GlobalWebIndex. The internet and related technologies are literally taking over the world and it's impossible today to become truly financially wealthy without embracing some form of technology.

Having technology work for you is a wise thing to do.

Put it into action

You need to utilize the potential of technology to drive your wealth creation and push you towards your financial goals. This can be achieved in a combination of three ways:

1. Create internet-based products and services
   - Think about what you could create and sell – from a series of apps to an internet-based service.
   - Consider different business models such as subscription as well as transactional.
   - What business is there a need for that's not currently being offered online?
2. Use the internet to run a business and grow your assets
   - Create an interactive business website using sites such as godaddy.com or register.com
   - Sell online using sites such as shopify.com, etsy.com and amazon.com
   - Find clients through referral websites or using client referral software solutions such as those offered by referralcandy.com
   - Source suppliers through sites such as oberlo.com, kompass.com and alibaba.com
   - Manage and track your wealth and assets using online applications provided by your bank, stockbroking firm or financial advisor.
   - Use a property management app such as landlordtracks.com to look after your property investments.
3. Use the internet to improve your life
   - Manage your time and productivity with apps such as todoist.com and the DayDayHabit habit tracker.
   - Keep de-stressed with apps such as calm.com and thinkpacifica.com
   - Use the cloud, Office 365 online and webmail to enable you to work from anywhere.

EXPECT BLACK SWAN MOMENTS

'Every so often, the markets do something that was never in the textbooks. Something so crazy a new textbook will be written about it.'

From Leicester City winning the 2016 English Premier League soccer title to the 2008 financial crash, things always happen that nobody expects. Named after the discovery that not all swans are white – something thought impossible by Europeans until they landed in Australia, that is – black swans are those unpredictable events that happen with alarming predictability, such as entire companies, banks, investment funds, currencies and countries collapsing, often in a single day:

- The failure of financial institutions such as Long-Term Capital Management, Citibank and Bank of Scotland.
- The 2000 dot-com bubble bursting, causing many tech firms to collapse.
- Scandals destroying companies such as Enron, WorldCom and Tyco.
- Terrible business strategies leading to firms like Kodak, Blackberry and Nokia almost disappearing.

It's easy to forget how many large and successful companies have disappeared or become much smaller, causing shareholders, bondholders, pension funds and banks to lose millions. What can you learn from this in your own pursuit of wealth?

Always assume that what 'will never happen' actually might.

69

Put it into action

Stop being surprised and shocked

The unexpected happens. The impossible becomes commonplace. You have to adapt and accept this reality and do what you can to avoid being caught out – or in other words, turn black swans into white swans.

How to turn black swans into white swans

The UK group Carillion saw a collapse in its share price during 2017, falling from a high of £2.38 down to about 12p. A major supplier of outsourced services to the UK government the company had seemed like a really well run and sound business. Financial writers in the media acted shocked and had you been holding shares in Carillion, you might have viewed its collapse as a black swan event.

I now read articles by some financial analysts who saw Carillion's collapse coming and sold their shareholdings in good time. No black swan for them, just another white swan swimming by. Would you have been able to spot Carillion's rising debts and falling profit margins and read the signs?

Whether you have a net wealth of £100,000 or a multi-billion-pound diversified global portfolio of investments, here's how to be prepared for future black swan moments:

- Accurately know what you are investing in. Know the fundamentals and know the markets you are buying the shares, properties or other assets in.
- Look for signs of potential problems. Work with outstanding financial advisors. Understand any investment you make and any asset you invest in. If in doubt get out.
- Diversify your portfolio. With a diverse portfolio, when a crisis happens, it doesn't destroy all of your wealth.

EMPLOY OTHERS TO ACHIEVE YOUR DREAMS

'I'd prefer to have 40 people working an hour a week for me than to work a 40-hour week alone.'

Here's a trick that very few people use that can massively boost your net worth: employ others to help you grow.

How much can you do by yourself? Even if you work 18 hours a day for 365 days a year, there's a limit to what you can achieve. You can't be in two places at once, you're not superhuman. Multi-tasking is over-rated and impossible to sustain. You could maybe do the equivalent of two people's jobs for a day or two, but not consistently and sustainably over time.

Despite all that, most self-employed people work alone as sole proprietors or independents with no one to help them. They're like de facto employees, doing all the work themselves. The only difference is that they invoice and earn fees, instead of taking home a salary.

So where does this leave you? Do you want to work alone or employ others to grow quicker? Which option would help you meet your life and financial goals?

> Extra pairs of hands can help accelerate your wealth creation.

70

Put it into action

Is there a business case for hiring?

Imagine you are a self-employed honey producer supplying local retailers. You want to expand the business but don't know where to start or how to make a decision. Ask yourself these questions:

- Do you want to invest more money and energy by growing the business with staff? How does this link to your financial goals and dreams?
- Is there potential to boost honey production? Could you sell the product to a larger client base, e.g. supermarkets? Is there flexibility in your business model afforded by having staff, for example opening a shop to sell your honey and related products?
- What is the profit margin per jar of honey? How much increased sales volume is needed to cover the cost of one potential employee, earning say $24,000 per annum?
- Could you hire someone part-time, on a zero-hours contract or on a commission-only basis? Could you take student interns?
- Are you happy to continue working in the honey business full-time? Or do you want to step back and leave an employee to take over the business?

Can you find what you need?

It is never easy finding great talent. Are you ready to find and attract the best possible candidates that you want to work with? Would this leave you time and energy for what's most important in your life?

TRUST YOUR INSTINCTS

'All the best decisions I've ever made have involved my gut instincts.'

'Intuition is everything' claims one of Spain's leading venture capitalists, Iñaki Arrola. An early investor in many of Spain's biggest tech start-ups, he shared, in a *Forbes* interview, an example of the power of intuition. He was socializing with a potential business partner, along with their spouses. *'After dinner, my wife said, "I don't know anything about numbers or potential partners, but this guy is going to cheat you." It was intuition. And he did.'*

I've learned the hard way that if your gut says something, you need to listen. If you have any nagging doubts about someone, be careful. If you're uncomfortable about a trading position, pause and reflect. If you have nagging doubts about an investment decision, review it.

In recent years, I've learned to listen to my gut and, since then, my decision making has improved. Achieving your financial goals takes both your head and your heart. Your head is your left-brain fact-based thinking and decision-making machine. Your heart is your gut feelings, instincts, sixth sense or intuition. Iñaki Arrola and his wife are not alone in putting their financial success down to listening to what their heart tells them. Even when it runs counter to hard facts and numbers.

> That little voice inside you is much more powerful than you can imagine.

Put it into action

Make space for your intuition

You can't hope to have any moments of intuition if you spend your days running from one task to another, your head filled with a thousand thoughts and anxieties. Give your gut feeling the chance to be heard by taking time to relax and slow down. Be present. Don't worry about yesterday or tomorrow. Instead allow random thoughts and feelings to enter your mind. The flashes of inspiration that come into your head in your quiet moments may surprise you and they might be the difference between winning or losing money on an investment.

Join the likes of Bill Gates in exploring the benefits of meditation. In a recent blog post, he shared how meditation has helped him improve his focus and be more at ease with the emotions and thoughts he's feeling at any moment. Try exploring meditation apps such as *Headspace* and *the Mindfulness App*.

Get better at judging people

As you grow your wealth, you will have to spend more time making decisions about other people, whether it's future employees, business and investment partners or suppliers. Be like Iñaki Arrola and his wife. Allow yourself to sense how you feel about another person. Do you feel comfortable with them and OK with their personality and behaviours? We all judge people within seconds of meeting them and the more time you can spend with them, the more thorough your assessment will be. Ask yourself if they seem like someone you can trust and work with.

THE PAST DOES NOT PREDICT
THE FUTURE

'The future owes nothing to the past or the present.'

You're more likely to invest in something if you've previously made a profit from a similar investment, even if evidence suggests it won't do well again. Investors call this *behaviour reinforcement*. University of California academics Brad Barber and Terrance Odean showed that we are more likely to subscribe for shares in an upcoming IPO (or initial public offering) if we've made a nice profit on another recent IPO, whatever the actual merits of the new IPO and company behind it. We're blinded by the past success.

Similarly, you have to beware of relying too much on graphs and tables of past performance showing historical data for anything you're interested in, from mutual funds, housing markets, and metals to stock market indices and individual shares, bonds and other assets. Market prices often appear to move in very predictable ways. An example might be a stock price rising in line with its moving average trendline. Or when a stock price does not fall lower than previous low points (called support levels). Beware of becoming comfortable. You never actually know when an asset's price will rise or fall to levels which are out of line with history, falling below its 5- or 10-year moving average trendlines or acting in ways you cannot foresee if relying upon historical charts and past data.

> Letting go of just focusing on the past takes effort and practice.

Put it into action

Take the past with a pinch of salt

It can be very reassuring to base your investment decisions on prices charts showing how well the asset you want to buy has been rising in recent quarters or years. Your bank's relationship manager, or your financial advisor, might also think it's a winner. But form your own views. Do your own reading and research and seek second opinions if necessary.

Repeat in moderation

Don't throw lots of money in one direction just because of past successes. Be cautious when you want to repeat an investment while still holding the first. This potentially doubles your exposure to the investment turning sour.

Always limit how much money you put it any one investment and don't throw all your spare money into an investment just because it's done well in the past. Treat each investment decision as a distinct standalone investment opportunity.

KNOW THE TRADE-OFFS

'Every choice is a trade-off. Successful people know this and always choose wisely.'

Life is all about trade-offs. You choose one career over another, one business partner instead of someone else, you agree to spend the week helping one client, forcing you to turn down the chance of working for another. You make these choices all the time because you, your time and money can't be in two places at once.

A trade-off, or opportunity cost as it's sometimes known, is a very important concept to understand when building wealth. The idea is that once you've invested your money in one option, it's no longer available to simultaneously invest in anything else. If you choose option A, you lose the benefits of option B.

Sometimes, it seems simple, but life is never that straightforward. You could put your career on hold to study for an Executive MBA at a top business school, but the job and salary prospects post MBA have to be balanced with what you sacrifice in career trajectory, remuneration and costs to get it.

> Don't underestimate the opportunity costs of any decision. Think about what you could lose by choosing one option over another.

Put it into action

Keep opportunity costs to a minimum and keep the bigger picture of your financial needs and goals in mind when making decisions today.

Don't ignore obvious opportunity costs

Sometimes you might not notice a high opportunity cost right in front of you. As an example, be careful of holding onto debts when you could pay them off from available funds. Suppose you have a credit card balance of $10,000 for which you are charged an equivalent of 18% interest annually while at the same time you're holding more than $10,000 in investments earning, before tax, about 6–8% per year on average. Are you comfortable living with this opportunity cost? Does it make sense to hold all of your 6% return investment, instead of liquidating part of it to pay off your high 18% interest debt?

Let go of under-performers

There's no point holding under-performing investments when you could sell them and use the funds for more profitable investing. For example, if you own an investment property that's hard to rent out, you are effectively holding an asset, perhaps with a mortgage to pay off, with no income coming in. Instead you could sell and invest in a property that would be easier to rent out, remembering to factor into the decision the potential house price appreciation in both locations.

SEEK THE HELP OF MENTORS

'Treasure anyone who will take the time to show you the way and warn you about the obstacles and hurdles ahead.'

Mentoring is defined by the European Mentoring and Coaching Council as a 'developmental process involving a transfer of skill or knowledge from a more experienced person to a less experienced person'. If you've ever been mentored before, you'll know it's typically done through a combination of teaching, sharing and role modelling.

The list of ways a mentor can help is endless. They might give you advice on where to study, how to understand something you've come up against, how to find a new job, how to succeed at work, how to invest, or how to get on with a difficult boss. It's growing in popularity too, especially in the workplace. New employees are often given a more experienced colleague to act as their mentor to help them settle into the job and understand how to succeed in the company.

The power of getting direct access to someone's own experiences is quite profound – even more so than reading it in a book or watching a video clip. When you're being mentored, you can have deep and meaningful two-way conversations. You can probe and double check and ask clarifying questions.

Finding a mentor with energy, passion and enthusiasm might be just the thing you need to launch your wealth creation plans.

Put it into action

Spend time with successful role models

If you really want to know how to become a millionaire, why not ask one to share their experiences with you? They're not that hard to find – at the last count, there were globally over 42 million millionaires, according to a 2018 report by Credit Suisse.

So you may not be in a position to rock up to a multi-millionaire's house and say, *'Please can you be my mentor?'*, and you might not be ready for a networking event on Richard Branson's Necker Island, but you can ask around your community for an introduction.

When you find a possible mentor, explain to them what your aspirations are and how you are hoping they can help you. Build up trust and rapport and if possible, try to meet face to face, on a regular basis. Thank them by buying coffee or lunch.

Learn online

It's not the same as sitting down one to one, but face-to-face meetings aren't always possible. Fortunately, there is much to learn on the web. There are many sites dedicated to providing mentoring style advice, and that includes helping people like you who want to achieve their financial goals and build up their wealth. Some sites have paid memberships and link you up over the web with a mentor:

- http://wealthmentors.com/
- https://financialmentor.com/
- https://dollarbillionaire.com/

Attend events filled with experts

'Mentworking' is a recently coined term that combines networking and being mentored. The idea is to find and attend networking events that give you a chance to meet potential mentors. Get yourself invited to high-net worth events, sign up for senior leadership talks or go along to entrepreneur seminars. Make an effort to put yourself in the room with people you want to emulate.

TIMING IS EVERYTHING

'I have never met anyone who can always tell when markets will fall or rise.'

Most investors have a bad track record with timing. The fact is, it's hard to buy and sell at exactly the right time. The annual financial returns of individual or retail investors typically lag behind those of managed funds – by as much as 1.4% per annum according to one US study by Morningstar Inc.

Not all individual investors fare worse than large managed funds, but those that do typically get one thing wrong: they jump in and out of investments at the wrong times, often selling before the prices have stopped rising.

In reality though, professionals only fare a little better than you and I because it's hard for *any* investor to perform better than the average returns of a market. Back in 2015, the *Financial Times* reported that over the last 30 years, the average investor had made an annual return of only 3.79% compared with the overall market return (based on the S&P 500 Index) of 11.6% per annum. Sounds to me like poor investing by the average investor.

In 2017 *The Economist* stated that it is hard for individual investors to select fund managers who will outperform their peers. There's certainly a trend among investors to move away from using fund managers and instead invest directly in tracker and index funds that passively track benchmark indices such as the FTSE100 and S&P 500. Passive funds also typically charge lower fees than active or exchange traded funds.

Unless you're convinced that you have perfect timing, it might make sense to consider some other strategies.

> Accept that it is not possible to accurately predict how markets will move.

Put it into action

Adopt a 'dollar-cost averaging' strategy

Stop trying to time the market. It's very hard, even for professionals, to know when to enter and when to leave. Instead if you're investing in a particular asset class or product, be consistent and invest an equal amount each month. Given price movements, some months you'll be able to buy more when the price is low and less when the price rises.

You can invest like this in anything that's actively traded: funds, gilts, T-bills, bonds, individual stocks or other assets such as gold. Over time you are buying at a range of market prices and the chances are you'll make better returns than if you were jumping in and out of the market like a typical individual investor. This is called 'dollar-cost averaging'.

As an example, assume you invest $500 every month and the average annual return of the asset/ fund over 20 years is 6%. In two decades' time, you will have amassed $232,175.55. Check this calculation out for yourself at the website planetcalc.com. Input the monthly amounts you might invest along with the expected annual % return. Do remember that these are pre-tax rates of returns.

You might prefer to invest an initial lump sum and add it when you have any surplus cash, in which case you could invest the money into a fund or pension scheme (such as your 401(k) plan if you are in the US). Do not touch the money, simply leave it to grow.

Funds are a good bet for regular investing

Find a fund with a good track record, ideally with lower fees and costs. In the UK, you could use the *Financial Times*' Fund Comparison Tool to help with your choices. Consider investing in tracker and index funds. These are passive funds that are linked to market indices. They tend to have lower fees. Do watch out for 'tracker error' though, which sometimes occurs when a fund doesn't accurately track the index it's meant to mirror.

LIVE A HEALTHY LIFESTYLE

'Break your bad habits, and you can gain so much extra time.'

Nobody ever got rich sitting around watching TV. An entrepreneur called Andrew Ferebee interviewed 400 wealthy people in the US and found that they watch TV on average for less than an hour a day. This compares to the average person's daily viewing pattern of about four hours a day in both the US and the UK, according to Statista data. Think about this for a minute. Financially successful people are finding an extra three hours a day for productive tasks while everybody else is being a couch potato.

There are similar statistics for time spent on social media, and playing computer and video games. Most people simply misuse their time on wasteful activities. Wean yourself away from bad habits – including staying off the smartphone – and you've given yourself the gift of time. Possibly quite a lot of it.

The same applies to general health too. On average, wealthy people exercise more, eat more healthily and sleep better than the typical person. Various studies bear this out as well as their own observations; Richard Branson has written about the benefits of exercise and how it keeps the brain functioning well while Jeff Bezos has spoken about getting eight hours of sleep a night.

To make money, you need to be creative, innovative and ready to work hard.

Put it into action

Ditch the screen

To build wealth, you need to keep yourself sharp, focused and alert while also being calm and able to keep your emotions under control. To achieve all of this you need to adopt certain habits. Starting today, you are going to radically cut your screen time and instead:

Eat intelligently every day

Eating healthily gives you a more positive mindset and more energy. In a 2015 study in the *British Journal of Health Psychology*, participants had their food consumption and their feelings and behaviours monitored for over two weeks. The study found that a diet comprising plenty of fruits and vegetables correlated to increased happiness and life satisfaction. It also found that such a diet might contribute to higher curiosity and creativity.

Exercise as much as possible

Countless studies show the importance of physical exercise to your overall health and well-being. Look no further than the 2013 US study in the journal *Psychology and Aging* which found that increased physical activity is linked to improved cognitive performance.

Sleep well and meditate

Only a very small number of people can function well on less than seven hours' sleep a night. It's time to start getting enough sleep – and ideally that means going to bed early and getting up early to give you the mental and emotional alertness and balance you need.

IT'S NOT THE END OF THE WORLD

'When you think you're facing catastrophe, ask yourself: is this going to matter in ten years' time?'

In a study reported by *The Journal of Nervous and Mental Disease*, 72 adults who lost their retirement savings in a bank fraud were monitored over time. Within 20 months of the loss, 29% suffered major depression compared with 2% in a normal population. In another study reported in the *Journal of Health Economics*, participants who lost savings in the 2008 stock market crash showed increased feelings of depression and use of antidepressant medication.

The average investor is very badly affected by major financial losses. Devastated would be a better description. How would you cope if you lost all your wealth or your pension fund collapsed? These things do happen, and before you know it, you can be back at square one. Imagine having to come out of retirement to go back to work or take on a second job, downsizing your home or cutting back on your lifestyle.

Hard as it may seem, it's best to accept that you will face setbacks on the way. Devastating as it seems now, there aren't many things in life that still matter in ten years' time.

Remember that if you've built something once, you can always do it again.

Put it into action

Don't sweat the small (or big) stuff

So how do you become the kind of person who can take this stuff in your stride? I can't simply tell you not to sweat the small stuff – having your home repossessed or losing all your wealth in a stock market crash hardly count as 'small stuff'. The issue is how not to sweat any stuff, big or small.

In the face of a major financial loss, you need to move forward and continue with your life positively, rebuilding your wealth from scratch if you choose to. The secret is resilience and focus; being emotionally grounded, and maintaining a positive attitude.

Money isn't everything. That's easy to say when you have it, not so easy when you're destitute. But it's true. It's not everything. Find your own balanced view about wealth and remember, as you build it up, to appreciate all aspects of your life so that if one day you lose a large chunk of your wealth, your life doesn't come to a standstill.

READ THE T&CS

'Some really annoying details get hidden in the small print.'

Ever had one of those *'if only I'd read the investment terms'* moments? We're inundated every day with terms and conditions, contracts, and agreements. They come via the post, email and within phone apps. When is the last time you actually read any of them? Do you even read the big important ones like your mortgage agreement, travel insurance terms, car lease agreement or life insurance contract?

The fact is, life is much sweeter if you can get by without reading the paperwork, but it can cost you – in both money and stress – if you don't. You might think your overdraft is cost effective, but have you checked on the rate and fees outlined in the agreement to make sure? You might want to settle your mortgage early, but do you have any idea what the early redemption fees set out in the loan paperwork look like?

Get into the habit of reading the paperwork, or at least skimming it to understand the kind of penalty rates and fees that can come as a surprise down the line. You'll soon get used to the kind of things you're looking for and be primed to pick up on those hidden extras. Take a mental note of each section or heading and make sure you know the numbers, the fees, penalties and timeframes.

With important paperwork, consider asking someone else, perhaps a lawyer or accountant, to check the details for you.

Reading terms and conditions can be so tedious and boring – but can be the difference between financial success and failure.

Put it into action

Caveat emptor (let the buyer beware)

It's so easy to get burned by not reading the small print. Remember, knowledge is power. Take time today to check some essential financial documents:

- Are you clear what your medical insurance covers?
- Does your credit card provide an extra 12 months of warranty when used to buy white goods etc.?
- Does a non-disclosure agreement with a potential investor tie your hands too much?
- With your income protection policy, are benefits payable when you are unable to pursue only your 'own' occupation or no occupation at all?
- Is the free travel insurance from your bank really worth it?
- Does your shareholder agreement give away too much control to others?
- For your house insurance to cover you against break-ins, do you need certain brands of locks?
- Does your holiday insurance cover everything you will do while you're away?
- What is missing from the list of insured critical illnesses?
- Does your income protection insurance policy have too many exceptions?

Cooling-off periods

Pause if you need time before signing and agreeing to something. Once you've committed, there's sometimes an opportunity to change your mind. In the UK, a company selling you financial products (such as ISAs, insurance, pension etc.) must provide clear information in a key features or key investor information document, including about your right to cancel the product, the timeframes, and any fees for doing so.

In the UK, only deal with financial institutions authorized by the Financial Conduct Authority so that you can take complaints to the Financial Ombudsman Service. Other countries have similar protections in place.

PUT YOUR EGGS INTO MANY BASKETS

'There's no single basket safe enough to protect all your eggs, all of the time.'

Imagine you've invested all of your money in London properties and are using Airbnb to create a continuous rental income stream, 365 days a year. All's going well until the '90-night rule' planning authority restriction is enforced which only allows London properties to be let out for 90 days per year. Added to this, London property prices have fallen. You've metaphorically put all of your eggs in one basket and now you're paying the price. It's very tempting to keep things simple – all your money with one bank, investing in only a small number of companies, owning properties in the same area – but it's very dangerous.

With only one basket, you risk losing all your wealth. With a poorly diversified portfolio, one risk is not offset by another. When one asset declines in value or its rate of return falls, you have no counter acting assets – no investments that may hold their value and returns while others fall. The risk hasn't been diversified.

The ideal is to mix and match. To create an investment portfolio made up of assets that will not move together in the same direction at the same time. This kind of diversification recognizes two things:

• Everything carries risk, even super safe cash. In an extreme case, a country's economy can collapse, leading to hyper-inflation and money becoming worthless.
• Spreading your investments limits exposure to any single event such as the dollar falling, a company going bankrupt or an emerging market economy faltering.

If in doubt diversify and place your wealth in different areas.

Put it into action

Act like a professional fund manager

No one professional fund manager will hold the same portfolio as another; each has a different risk tolerance, clients, goals and aims. On average the typical UK retail investor holds a mixture of equities (stocks) (77%), bonds (fixed income) (33%) and residential property (30%), according to a survey by syndicateroom.com. In the US, a 2018 AAII Asset Allocation Survey found that individual investors hold, on average: stocks (34%), stock funds (31%), bonds (3%) and bond funds (12%), and cash (20%). These percentages move up and down all the time as investors and fund managers react to market changes.

Professionals carry out analysis and research to create optimal portfolios. They typically practise dynamic asset allocation which involves redistributing assets among various classes based on the probabilities of expected market prices and returns, compared to the risks in each asset class. As a result, their investments yield multiple income streams. It takes time, expertise and confidence to get it right – that's why they're the professionals. Your challenge is to decide whether you have what it takes to mimic them, maintaining a good mix of assets and redistributing as needed to keep an optimal balance, or to take the easier option, invest in funds and leave your fund managers to manage your money. If you have any doubts at all, you should do the latter.

CUT YOUR LOSSES

'As soon as you realize you're digging a hole, stop and get out.'

Many investors have the habit of selling winners too soon and holding onto losers for too long, often not selling even when the price is falling before their very eyes. This is known as loss aversion or the disposition effect – a pattern where investors tend to sell assets that have risen in value while keeping those that have fallen, preferring to cash in profits, often too early, while avoiding realizing any paper losses.

Recouping losses is statistically very hard. This is because of the nature of percentage changes. Consider the following example:

- You choose to hold onto a share that is falling in value that you originally bought for $900. You could have sold at any point, but you let it fall by 20% to a new market price of $720 (i.e. 900 × 0.8) before selling.
- To return to its original price, you might imagine the asset would simply have to rise in value by 20%? Wrong. When $720 rises by 20% it only comes to $864 (i.e. 720 × 1.2).
- To get back to the original value of $900, $720 has to increase by 25%. And making a 25% gain in any investment is a lot more effort than allowing it to fall by 20%.

When was the last time you cut your losses?

Put it into action

Be mentally ready to stop digging

When you're on a losing streak, forget the sunk costs – the effort and money invested. Forget the possibility of making back the loss. Instead concentrate on what you have to gain by cutting your losses, rather than what you have to lose. Work by Northwestern University psychologists Chin Ming Hui and Daniel Molden shows that the optimal approach when 'de-escalating your commitments to something', such as holding onto a loss-making investment, is to look at the positive. Think of the freed-up cash as something you can now invest in profitable assets.

Use tools to help

With shares, you can place stop-loss orders with your stockbroker or in your trading software. These are instructions to sell the stock when it falls below a certain price designed to limit your losses. In the example of the $900 share, you could have set a stop-loss order for 10%. Meaning the stockbroker would sell when the price reaches $810 (i.e. $900 × 0.9), thereby limiting your loss to only $90 per share.

Unfortunately, this isn't fool-proof. Sometimes the price falls so fast, with no buying volume, that your stockbroker or your trading software won't be able sell around the 10% loss mark. That's just a fact of life and it just goes to show that there really is no risk-free investment.

Differentiate long-term holdings

You can approach your longer-term investments, those assets you choose to hold through the ups and downs of cycles, differently. With these, for example the monthly contributions you make to any funds, you don't need to worry about cutting your losses. The exception of course is when catastrophe strikes and one of the companies you're investing in hits the wall, its share price collapsing, bankruptcy looming. It would be prudent at this point to offload all your shares as soon as possible.

INVEST SUSTAINABLY

'How can you sit on a pile of gold when people around you are struggling to get by?'

Do you want to grow your wealth and have a positive impact on the world at the same time? Ethical investing is rising in popularity, especially amongst the young. According to Morgan Stanley research, 82% of high-net-worth millennials are interested in sustainable and ethical investment approaches, compared with 45% of all high-net-worth individuals.

You may have read about sustainable investing, impact investing or ethical investing. More and more of our investment decisions and allocations are based on these criteria. Collectively, such investing is referred to as sustainable and impact investing (SII).

There are plenty of examples around: UBS's 2018 Investor Watch global survey of wealthy investors found that 39% have some sustainable investments within their portfolios; in 2017 Japan's Government Pension Investment Fund, which is the world's largest pension fund, went into partnership with the World Bank Group to promote sustainable investments; and Norway's sovereign-wealth fund stated in 2017 that it would dispose of all its oil and gas investments, which together total about £27 billion.

There are many forums, events and bodies with an SII focus, such as the Global Impact Investing Network. The growth of industries such as those in energy efficiency, clean water and sustainable agriculture is constantly creating new SII investment opportunities.

> Sustainable investing is a sector to look out for, both for your wallet and your conscience.

Put it into action

Place your money with sustainability advocates

According to Schroders, sustainability advocates are those institutional investors who've committed to increasing the share of sustainable investments in their portfolios. A third of all investors surveyed in 2018 by Schroders fell into this category. In addition, many fund or portfolio managers have signed up to the United Nations' Principles for Responsible Investment.

Invest in sustainable funds

Place your capital in 'socially responsible indices' such as the MSCI KLD 400 Social Index or the FTSE4Good UK Index. They are made up of companies with strong sustainability and ethical profiles; companies that are high in so-called environmental, social and governance (ESG) factors.

Are you OK with lower returns?

There is evidence that when taking an SII approach, your investment returns might be lower than otherwise. A 2018 *Financial Times* article reported that the Norwegian state pension fund estimated that it had lost nearly 2% of return over the last ten years due to not investing in so-called ethically challenged companies in fields such as weapons manufacturing and coal mining.

But lower returns may not be inevitable. Other data shows that returns may actually even be better than for conventional investments. The UK's *Money Week* magazine reported in 2018 that during the past five years the FTSE4Good UK Index returned 60% (with dividends reinvested) compared with the FTSE 100's return of 51%.

NEVER TOO LATE TO START

'Age is just a number. As we live longer, we have more time and opportunity to fulfil every imaginable goal and dream.'

It's never too late to start something great:

- Mahathir Bin Mohamad became Malaysia's Prime Minister in his 90s.
- The Nobel Prize winner Jens Skou began learning computer coding in his 70s.
- Vera Wang waited until her 40s before starting her own fashion empire.
- Harland Sanders started KFC in his 60s.
- John Pemberton created Coca-Cola in his 50s.
- Ray Kroc founded McDonald's in his 50s.
- Robin Chase was in his 40s when he created Zipcar.

Evidence suggests that starting a business in later life increases your chances of success. In a study entitled 'Age and high-growth entrepreneurship', researchers, headed by MIT's Pierre Azoulay, found that a 50-year-old creator of a start-up is nearly twice as likely to achieve high levels of business growth compared with a 30-year-old founder. Experience and wisdom seem to count for something.

With saving and investing, it's always better to start as soon as possible, but starting later can still yield good returns. Suppose you can save $1,000 per month; assuming an average annual return of 3%, let's see how much you would have, before tax, by the time you reach 65:

Age when saving starts	Total amount deposited	Total interest earned	Total bank balance
20	$540,000	$603,000	$1.14 million
30	$420,000	$323,000	$743,000
40	$300,000	$147,000	$447,000
50	$180,000	$48,000	$228,000

Put it into action

Keep those business ideas rolling in

Today's culture and media are obsessed with youth, but it doesn't matter whether you're a 30-year-old struggling on a low salary, a 40-year-old recently made redundant, a 50-year-old who's taken early retirement or a 65-year-old on a State pension, you still have plenty to offer.

Hold onto your dreams, whether it's dreams of starting your own business or creating financial freedom for you and your family. Young people have energy on their side, but when you're older you have experience and wisdom. Either way you can succeed as an entrepreneur, it all depends on your mindset, belief, determination and desire. Forget your age and act energetic and keen. The Azoulay study found that the average age of start-up founders is 42, rising to 45 for the top 0.1% of the fastest-growing start-ups.

Start saving and investing today

Same with saving and investing. Keep an eye out for special deals for the old. Until a couple of years ago, over-65s in the UK could buy so-called *pensioner bonds*. You were able to invest up to £20,000 per person, or £40,000 per couple. The annual interest rates were good: 2.8% on a one-year bond and 4% on a three-year one. Check out what's available today.

BE READY FOR RAINSTORMS

'Growing up in England, I learned to always carry an umbrella. I have taken this learning into my financial investing.'

In a life-or-death situation, you can call the emergency services, but what do you do in the event of losing your income? What if you unexpectedly lose your job, your business or your investments? What have you got in reserve?

We've already seen how little most people save. It's even worse than you imagine. The UK internet bank First Direct carried out a survey and discovered that 7% of the population have total savings of less than £250, which First Direct estimated would enable someone to survive for five days based on average monthly household outgoings of £1,536.

How can you plan to build up your wealth if you can't even survive a week without earning any income? Truth is, it can be done but it's very stressful. What you really need is something to fall back on.

> You will regret trying to survive a rainy day without anything to keep you financially afloat.

Put it into action

Decide how much to have in your emergency piggy bank

Best practice suggests keeping enough in reserve to live on for at least a few months. To calculate this, you need to list your expenses and determine your essential monthly outgoings. Keep an emergency fund equivalent to at least three months of such expenses, ideally six if possible. Put this money into a separate savings account that pays interest, and that you can get access to if needed.

Aim to own the roof over your head

You can't concentrate on success-focused goals if you're going to bed with the threat of homelessness looming over you. It is much easier to survive difficult moments when you own your own home outright, avoiding panic attacks about being unable to pay the rent or mortgage.

Seek impartial advice

If you're unsure about how to manage your money and savings, seek impartial help. In the UK, I would suggest contacting the Money Advice Service (www.moneyadviceservice.org.uk) which was set up by the government. It offers free and independent advice on topics such as how to create an emergency fund of savings. In the US, go to www.usa.gov/money.

UNDERSTAND IT OR GET OUT

'Be careful playing games with money. If you don't know the rules, you'll lose.'

One of Warren Buffett's key pieces of advice is never to invest in businesses you don't understand. The same applies to money. Never put it into anything – shares, derivatives and other financial products – you couldn't actually explain to someone else.

It can be a bit of a thrill doing something you don't fully understand. It can even lead to new and unexpected discoveries. But when your money is involved, excitement can easily turn to despair.

In terms of financial products, there are hundreds of them and many are difficult to understand. Sometimes even the names of the products are complicated which should serve as a warning in itself to steer clear of them; check out the *VelocityShares Daily Inverse VIX Short-Term exchange-traded note (XIV)*, an investment product Credit Suisse stopped from trading after it lost 93% of its value overnight.

You'll probably miss a few opportunities as a result – Buffett passed up the opportunity to be an early investor in Amazon and Google, but he doesn't regret his decision, and you won't either. Better to be safe and sound than hung out to dry.

'If you can't explain it simply, you don't understand it well enough.' (Albert Einstein)

Put it into action

Can you explain it in simple words?

Make it your rule of thumb to always be able to explain in simple terms to someone else what you're putting your money into. If you can't pass this simple test, you know what to do.

If you're planning to invest in a start-up business, make sure you understand the business model. It's not enough that someone else understands it. The founder of the company may be incredibly passionate, and it may be obvious that *they* understand it. But do *you* and can you explain it yourself?

If you're investing in financial products, don't rely on your bank's relationship managers extolling the high potential returns. They're paid to do that. Be especially wary when even they cannot explain in simple terms what they are trying to sell.

DON'T BE A HARE

'If you ignore the instructions before assembling the furniture, don't be surprised to find one leg is shorter than the other when you finish.'

Overconfidence in your ability is a common human trait. Psychologists Howard Raiffa and Marc Alpert call it the overconfidence effect and the results can be shocking. In a 2015 paper published in *Psychological Science*, three Cornell and Tulane academics concluded that having a high belief in their own knowledge led people to claim they knew things that were totally impossible or fictitious. In the study, participants confidently said they knew about and understood certain financial terms that the researchers had actually made up.

It's frightening to think that we often rely on confident people for guidance and advice. Research by Brad Barber and Terrance Odean has shown that lawyers, doctors and other professionals are prone to overconfidence and furthermore that men are often more overconfident than women. In one US study by Daniel Kahneman, four-fifths of entrepreneurs surveyed claimed that their businesses had a 70% or higher probability of succeeding – far higher than the reality in which only about 35% of small US start-ups survive more than five years.

The message is clear. Be aware of your levels of confidence and be open to the possibility that you may be suffering from the overconfidence effect. Remember it's the Tortoise, not the Hare, who wins the race. The Hare is overconfident, takes his eye off the ball and gets beaten to the finishing line by the slow-moving Tortoise.

What will it take for you to calm down your level of overconfidence and become more humble?

Put it into action

Avoid excessive trading

Researchers have found that overconfident investors trade more often than others do. In 'Trading is hazardous to your wealth', Barber and Odean showed that excessive trading leads to high fees and costs that can easily wipe out almost all gains made. They also found that overconfident traders timed their trades badly compared with their more cautious counterparts.

Plan better for retirement

Avoid being too confident in how much money you're going to need in retirement. Better to be safe than sorry on this one and assume you'll need more than you think. In the Employee Benefit Research Institute's 2017 Retirement Confidence Survey, 60% of respondents were confident or overconfident they'd be able to save enough to afford a comfortable retirement, but in the same survey only 41% admitted to having calculated how much they'd need to be comfortable. Many of these did not fall into the 60%. Over half said that their healthcare costs were higher than they'd expected, supporting other evidence that retirees are overconfident in having enough money to live on.

Don't blindly believe the Hares

In a well-known study in 2006, researcher James Montier surveyed 300 professional fund managers on their performance. Nearly 100% of them felt that their performance was average or better than average when in reality their funds represented a broad cross-section of performance. We're all fallible – just be aware that even the professionals can also get it wrong.

EXPLORE SAFE HAVENS CAREFULLY

'There are no calm harbours in today's choppy oceans.'

When you think about protecting your money during troubled times, what do you think of as a safe haven? Gold, cash, Swiss francs, Japanese yen, UK gilts, US Treasury Bills, silver, Chinese yuan, property? All of these have been regarded at one time or another as stable assets. For a while even Bitcoin was viewed as super safe, well, at least until its price collapsed.

Safe havens are important because while other assets fall in price, safe haven products hold their value, or rise as demand increases. It sounds very simple and for years the tendency for these assets to hold value has held true. In recent years the results have been more mixed.

Gold is the ultimate safe haven. It's always been viewed as the safest place to put your wealth. Its value can't be manipulated by interest rates. It's a physical asset that can't be printed at will like money. But its price, normally quoted per ounce, has been very volatile recently. During 2018, gold's market price per ounce hit a high of US$1,356 before falling as low as US$1,175, a decline of 13%. Add to that the fact that you can't earn a return on holding gold, you can only hope that its value rises.

Other supposed safe haven assets have also shown mixed performance. In fact, it's been noted that since the 2008 financial crisis, neither gold, the US dollar nor the Japanese yen have been particularly stable. So what is an investor to do?

> Investing in a world where there are no obvious safe havens is not easy.

Put it into action

Do the same due diligence as for any other asset

If traditionally safe haven assets are no longer holding their value in the way you'd expect, is there anywhere left to safely park your wealth?

The answer is simply to treat safe havens like any other potential asset you'd invest in. In other words, not specially at all. You can no longer blindly invest your money in safe havens when a recession or global crisis looms. Instead think of assets like gold, UK gilts or Swiss francs as some of the more stable investments – but recognize that none of them is risk-free, and might fall in value.

As with gold, physical safe havens such as precious metals offer no return, while the deposit interest on cash deposits is low. The returns (or yields) on government bonds such as US 30-year Treasury Bills, German ten-year bunds and UK ten-year gilts are also low and you can't hold them in expectation of their market prices rising, to give you capital gains.

None of these is a sure bet but you should hold them as part of a mixed portfolio - a strategy known as hedging your bets, or balancing differing risks and rewards. An easier alternative is to invest in funds that have a portfolio mix that suits your needs.

RE-IGNITE YOUR CHILD-LIKE CURIOSITY

'I used to make fun of adults who acted like children. Now I try to hire them!'

The New York Times columnist Adam Bryant once asked 70 CEOs and other senior business leaders one question: 'What qualities do you see most often in those who succeed?' The top answer might surprise you. It was passionate curiosity.

And a survey of 3,000 professionals, reported in the *Harvard Business Review* in 2018, revealed that 92% of those surveyed claimed that it is those who are curious who bring new ideas to teams – that curiosity in a team improves people's motivation and performance.

When passion and curiosity are combined, you have people with an intense fascination for everything in their lives. So many innovations and business successes have come from passionately curious people. Today's tech giants – Facebook, Alibaba, Google etc. – are the result of founders with these qualities, driven to innovate and create solutions, often for problems that didn't even exist yet.

Most people don't make time to be curious. They ignore things that highly successful people find intriguing. The writer Paul C. Brunson described a conversation with the Turkish billionaire Enver Yücel, marvelling at Yücel's curiosity about things others might dismiss such as the relative heights of roadside curbs in Washington DC and Istanbul. But the point is that it's through this kind of passionate curiosity that the most unexpected and untapped ideas emerge. Ideas that might be financially lucrative. Do you know anyone like Yücel or how could you be more like him?

> Curiosity is something that can be learned and mastered through practice.

Put it into action

Build up your wealth based on questions, not answers

Google's former CEO, Eric Schmidt, once said that Google is run based on asking questions, not on finding answers. When facing challenges and opportunities, express your curiosity through asking questions. Encourage those around you to also ask questions and not to accept the obvious. Focus on things like: *'Why not?', 'What if?', 'What might be possible?'*

Wealth comes from creating value that others are willing to pay for and value is often the result of someone being curious, of asking and exploring questions, finding some untapped value. Polaroid's shareholders became very wealthy thanks to an inventor, Edwin Land, who listened to his daughter. The two had been taking photos, and she asked her father: *'Why do we have to wait for the picture?'*

Remain keenly curious, even as you get older

41% of millennials understand cryptocurrencies, compared with just 18% of baby boomers, according to a 2018 Legg Mason study. In another 2018 survey, this time by YouGov, 44% of millennials said that they expected cryptocurrencies to be widely used in the next ten years, compared with only 34% of generation X and 29% of baby boomers.

Younger people are more naturally open-minded, so stay young and don't allow your years of experience to close your eyes to what's happening around you. You don't know everything and you should always be willing to leave your comfort zone, be open-minded and explore.

GROW YOUR WEALTH IN A VUCA WORLD

'Today's high-speed ever-changing world seems to be accelerating.'

If you're investing today, you're doing it in a very unstable and high-speed world. We live in a VUCA environment, which means that you can expect:

- Volatility
- Uncertainty
- Complexity
- Ambiguity

Volatility right now can be quite extraordinary, with markets rapidly rising and falling, sometimes in seconds:

- In October 2016, the value of sterling dropped more than 6% in two minutes against the US dollar.
- June 2017, the price of the largest cryptocurrency after Bitcoin, Ethereum, dropped in a few minutes from over US$300 to as low as 10 US cents.
- The Swiss franc rose 40% against the euro in a matter of seconds back in January 2015.
- In 2013, prices on Singapore's Stock Exchange collapsed in minutes by up to 87%.

Flash crashes like these are increasingly common due to the complexity of modern-day trading on financial markets caused by high-frequency trading, complicated futures trading, black-box trading, over-reliance on software algorithms, and of course the occasional bit of market manipulation.

Not too long ago, before widespread internet and emails and real-time online systems for trading, nothing happened in seconds. Today thousands of trades can occur simultaneously in milliseconds.

Added to this, you have to deal with a deluge of information and data to the point where googling advice on a market, trade or company is likely to leave you none the wiser. Some sources will say the answer is black, others will say it's white. Unfortunately, you're just going to have to get used to grey.

Only invest in what you understand and pay for advice if you need it.

88

Put it into action

Rely less on your own trading skills

Given the greyness of information and extreme volatility of the markets, it's becoming harder to rely on your own skills to be a successful individual retail investor. There's a growing argument that it's best to hold most of your financial market investments in funds managed by professionals with better systems, research and timing.

There's also a trend towards holding more physical assets, such as property, gold and antiques – something some financial analysts refer to as a back to basics approach. The beauty of assets like this is that they're not going to fall in value by 80% in five seconds. This is a good strategy for countering the high-speed algorithm-based trading in the City and on Wall Street.

Keep up your momentum

One of the effects of our increasingly complex financial world is that it's easy to become confused, fragmented and lose focus. You hope your investments will do OK, and become paralysed when they don't. Remember the advice from earlier in the book: only invest in what you understand and pay for professional advice if you need it.

I also want to share with you a very simple equation which was created by the social researcher and author Michael McQueen. It states that:

Momentum (the process of moving forward and growing) = (Activity + Focus) × Consistency

To build momentum with your wealth, in spite of the volatility, uncertainty, complexity and ambiguity around you, isn't easy. You need to:

- be clear on your financial activities, the products, assets and markets you want to invest in
- give enough focused time and attention to your wealth
- be consistent in your choices and actions and don't allow the noise and confusion around you to throw you off course.

BE AN EXPERT NEGOTIATOR

'Everything is open to negotiation.'

You'll never become wealthy unless you learn to negotiate. Sometimes negotiation is about pushing hard to secure what you need, sometimes it means compromising, and sometimes it means simply walking away. You've probably already negotiated more than you think when you bought or sold a property, agreed fees and terms with your bank or stockbroker, signed an employment contract, agreed a salary increase or details of a job promotion.

One of the world's most successful dealmakers and negotiators is Stephen Schwarzman. He is a co-founder and CEO of the Blackstone Group which he's led to become one of the world's largest private equity and investment firms, managing assets of over US$450 billion. He advises anyone negotiating to find their zone of fairness, in other words, the overlap of what you need and want with what the other party is hoping for. The skill is recognizing the overlap and agreeing on how to get there.

You're looking to find a balance in other words, and one of the best ways to do this is to make your own needs clear and at the same time to put myself in their shoes to understand the pressures on them. So get used to stating your position very precisely, saying for example: *'I need a 20% reduction in fees to be able to continue using your service'* or *'I'm looking for a timeframe of less than three months to close this deal, or I'll have to walk away.'* At the same time put yourself in their shoes to understand the pressures on them.

The hardest part of a negotiation is knowing when to walk away.

89

Put it into action

Practice makes perfect

Schwarzman has spent 40 years honing his skills. You may be nowhere near that. You'll feel like a novice at first, struggling to assert your needs and worrying about upsetting the other party. As you get more experienced, you'll become more comfortable finding agreement within the 'zone of fairness'.

Be ready to walk away

When you're caught up in a negotiation, it can be hard to keep sight of the point at which an agreement is unacceptable, when a price offer is too low, or when the percentage shareholding demanded in return for investment funds is too high. It is very hard to reach these points and say 'no' simply because you've probably invested so much to get there. It might be impossible to imagine *not* agreeing a deal. At these moments, step back and pause. Seek advice. Find a mentor to talk with.

Have a Plan B

What do you do if you can't reach an agreement? You need a Plan B. Roger Fisher and William Ury, members of the Harvard Negotiation Project, call it your BATNA or 'your best alternative to a negotiated agreement'. This is the second-best option for when you can't agree your preferred terms.

Write it down

Once you have reached an agreement, remember to document it. Just a short email is sometimes enough but the key is to have something in writing, and to share it with the other parties.

FOCUS ON YOUR EQ NOT IQ

'Given the choice, I will always opt to work with someone with high levels of emotional intelligence.'

Research consistently shows that the higher your EQ (emotional intelligence), the more successful you'll be.

- TalentSmart, a San Diego-based consultancy in the field of EQ, assessed a range of individuals against 34 important workplace skills. Their study concluded that emotional intelligence is the most important predictor of performance, explaining 58% of a person's success in their work.
- In another study spanning 45 years and reported in the *Journal of Research in Personality*, 80 scientists were assessed at the ages of 27 and 72. The research revealed that emotional and social abilities were more important than IQ in explaining the individual's creativity over their lifetime.
- A US study published in the *Journal of Vocational Behavior* in 2017 concluded that the higher a person's emotional intelligence, the higher their salary and degree of job satisfaction.

EQ comprises:

- your understanding, or self-awareness, of your own emotions, actions and feelings
- your ability to control, or self-manage, these emotions and actions
- your skill in being empathetic, putting yourself in other people's shoes – also called being socially aware
- your ability to manage how you interact and communicate with other people.

In recent years a number of the world's super-rich have spoken about its importance to their success, including Jack Ma, who noted in 2017 that you need great EQ to help you to work with people. The lesson here is that although it seems fluffy, you should never underestimate your ability to understand and manage your emotions as a key factor in your financial success.

EQ is an essential foundation for being able to create a life of financial success.

90

Put it into action

Understand how your EQ has impacted you

Reflect on moments in your life when your EQ has either helped or hindered you. By doing this you can understand what aspects of your emotional intelligence need to be better managed and developed. Take a moment to write down your most memorable 'EQ moments'. Have you for example become angry with a colleague or business partner, causing the relationship to sour? Have you got frustrated at a lower than expected bonus payment and decided to leave your job?

Learn from your past

You'll probably find lots of examples of where your emotions have been in the driving seat, rather than you controlling your EQ, and you can use these as lessons. It's important for you to master your emotions, not let them master you. That way you can make more thoughtful decisions and react to situations more calmly. This is where you start being an EQ expert.

Encourage others to master their emotions

There's little point in being emotionally intelligent if those around you are doing the opposite. Help people around you grow their EQ too. The last thing you want are outbursts, inappropriate words and actions negatively impacting your own finances and financial plans.

KEEP YOUR PAPERWORK IN ORDER

'When we mess up, lose things or forget things we only have our past selves to blame.'

If you want to be super successful, you need to be super organized. I once met a woman who had lost her winning lottery ticket. She'd spent days searching for it, finally deciding it had been thrown away by mistake. Last I heard, she was planning to contact the council to try to persuade them to search a local refuse site.

Even if you're not a lottery winner, forgetting about or losing paperwork can be costly. If you've ever mislaid an important business contract or shareholders agreement, or forgotten to submit a tax return on time and received a fine, you'll understand.

As you build up your assets, you'll have more paperwork to look after, increasing the possibility of overlooking an unpaid bill, unsigned contract or an agreement not submitted on time.

If you're very wealthy, you can leave all the organizing, paperwork and filing to others. If you don't have the luxury of employing assistants to manage everything or having professionals run a family office for you, you need to own this yourself.

This is your mantra: sort, file, act.

Put it into action

Have an organized workspace

Keep your workplace clean and organized. When your study or workstation is messy, it's harder to focus on one particular task at a time. A 2011 *Journal of Neuroscience* study by Princeton University researchers discovered that our brain's visual cortex becomes overwhelmed by irrelevant paperwork and objects, making it hard to complete tasks efficiently.

Keep a list of all the bills you expect to receive and ensure you do actually receive and pay them. For each of your investments, maintain a checklist and file of all the required paperwork. Note the things you need to submit, update or file and pay particular attention to deadlines such as when you should pay things like business rates or submit your tax return. Don't forget autopay payments; if you don't do anything about them, the autopay instructions will be automatically rolled over for another 12 months.

Use secretarial services

Depending on your available budget, you might consider paying someone to help you. It's easy to hire in secretarial services by the hour, getting exactly the admin support you need.

Make use of the internet

There are some excellent online tools to help you keep organized. Check out websites and apps such as:

- Expensify, Zoho Expense and Evernote which allow you to scan and manage expense receipts
- GnuCash, Buddi and AceMoney which are simple accounting/book-keeping systems.

Don't overlook emails, especially if they are the only form of communication you receive from your utility company, property management company or bank. Take a note of their contents, and print them out and file if you have to.

BE STEALTHY WITH YOUR WEALTH

'Showing off your wealth is like taking off your clothes, showing people your fat belly and saying:
"Look at this – it is filled with so much amazing food."'

Many of today's billionaires exhibit something called stealth wealth. They stay beneath the radar in their daily lives, they don't feel the need to be driven in the most expensive car or own the largest house in the road. Basically they don't let their immense wealth go to their heads.

- The founder of Ikea, Ingvar Kamprad, reportedly drives a 15-year-old Volvo and flies economy class.
- Apple's CEO, Tim Cook, lives in a relatively modest home in his Palo Alto neighbourhood filled with multi-million-dollar properties.
- One of the world's richest people, Carlos Slim, is reported to live in the same modest home he bought over 30 years ago and still drives himself to work.

Never flaunt your wealth. Arrogance isn't a good look on anyone. Be gentle when talking about your wealth and avoid making other people feel small and inadequate, but equally don't deny what you've achieved. You've worked hard and you've earned it.

In what way have you been showing off your wealth and finances?

92

Put it into action

Stay humble and grounded

There is never any reason to be embarrassed of becoming wealthy or wanting to enjoy your wealth through your lifestyle choices. It's OK to feel proud of being financially successful, but act in moderation. Be low key and humble or risk being used as a piggy bank by those close to you. Sharing is great, but if you're just constantly giving, your relationships will change and money will become the main bond of friendship, with jealousy bubbling just beneath the surface. No one wants that.

If you become too ostentatious it can single you out to people outside your immediate circle too. Before long you might find acquaintances, neighbours and even strangers wanting money from you, being over-friendly or making financial requests directly, or via those close to you. Probably the most common request you'll hear is being asked for a loan for a business idea. Talking start-ups can be fun but not if you're getting hit on constantly.

Have the courage to say no

You will never be able to please everybody who wants some of your wealth. On a regular basis think through who in your life you would like to help. Politely but firmly say no to requests from others. Develop a thick skin if needed to make this process a little easier.

Say yes to others with clarity and openness

With those you are willing to help, do so without making the other party beg, feel guilty or ashamed. Be very open with them about how much you are able to give. Clearly explain your expectations and whether the money is a gift or a loan. And remember, no showing off: give to others quietly, without any fanfare.

DO NOT BLAME OTHERS FOR YOUR LOSSES

'Take 100% responsibility for your financial life. To do otherwise will bring you constant agitation and bitterness.'

Never place the fault for your financial issues at the feet of other people:

- It's not the estate agent's fault that you didn't ask about the council tax band or property management fee when buying the apartment.
- It's not the broker's fault that the fund you invested in didn't return double digit growth.
- It's not the leasing firm's fault that they couldn't find tenants to pay above market rate rentals for your newly renovated property.
- It's not your boss's fault that you haven't been promoted and had a raise.
- It's not the new investor's fault that you didn't build more protection into your shareholder agreement, even though you sensed you needed it.

I once bought a house in Malaysia, without realizing that an apartment complex was about to be built at the back of my property. I couldn't believe that the property agent and lawyer had never mentioned it, but in truth I'd never asked, and the planning permission was submitted only during the purchase. No one was at fault but me. I'd never actually looked at the back of the property and thought, why is that land being cleared?

> When it comes to your own money, you're the only person who can take the credit – and the blame.

93

Put it into action

Don't look for scapegoats

Unless you have a gun to your head, you are solely responsible when signing and agreeing to anything. Deflecting responsibility onto others is a poor strategy and stressful. It only serves to alienate other people and holds you back from learning. You'll make mistakes. You don't know everything. But next time you'll come back wiser, and by then, hopefully, nothing will go wrong.

You can't change for the better if you never acknowledge the mistakes you make. When you take responsibility and ownership, amazing things happen. You become more resilient and confident, more careful in making financial choices. Ready to double check and check again when needed, always prepared to adjust or alter an earlier decision.

Don't get ripped off

Then again, if you've been cheated or mis-sold, you *can* legitimately blame someone else. There have been plenty of instances of professionals giving dishonest advice or pushing customers to buy products they don't need. Practise due diligence. Sense-check the advice given to you and get a second opinion if needed.

HAVE AN ANNUAL WEALTH CHECK

'When you neglect to care about your wealth, you will end up with the financial equivalent of tooth decay.'

Most of us go to the doctor or dentist every once in a while for a check-up. Your finances are no different. You need to regularly check in on the health of your savings and investments, rooting out any problems and fine tuning them to perfection. If you don't review your decisions, you have no way of knowing if they're still holding good.

It's incredible how we make important decisions and choices, and later forget all about them, but even more bizarre is the number of people who leave money in savings schemes and accounts only to forget it ever existed. In the UK there's even a dedicated website (www.mylostaccount.org.uk) to help people find long lost bank and building society accounts.

By carrying out a regular financial health check you can review not only the performance of your money but also the performance of those managing it. On the next page you'll find a step-by-step guide to how to perform a financial health check, and what to look out for.

It is no good going for your first wealth check only after you have experienced the financial equivalent of major tooth decay.

94

Put it into action

Perform an annual financial health check

How well has your money invested in funds performed?

Are the funds' returns beating comparable indices? In the UK, most funds would be compared to the FTSE100 index. Few funds beat the index every year but you should not stay with a fund that never exceeds its comparative index.

How much dividend income did you earn?

This is key if you rely on regular income from share invesntments. You're doing OK if you received at least 5p or 6p for every £1 invested in shares. But could you do better? For the year ahead, do you switch money from lower- to higher-paying dividend shares?

How has your mix of investments changed?

If shares have performed well this year, you may have gone from a portfolio with a 50:50 split of bonds and shares to a 70:30 split in favour of shares. Do you now re-balance this? From a risk perspective does your current portfolio suit your needs?

Are you making full use of tax savings schemes?

In the UK, are you maximizing the full allowance for placing your savings in tax-free Individual Savings Accounts (ISAs)? Also, be aware of other tax-efficient savings and investment schemes, that you may not be taking full advantage of.

Are there better fixed-term rates available?

Keep a note of when any fixed-term deposit period expires before it is auto-renewed and your money is trapped for another year. Explore if there are better options available.

Are your property investments being optimized?

Are your rental returns (pre- or post-tax) meeting your expectations? Are they comparable to market averages? Are the properties maintaining or growing in market value? Are the property management company's fees competitive?

PASS ON YOUR FINANCIAL TIPS

'I have learned so much from teaching others. As I share what I've learned, I'm astonished by the number of new insights I gain.'

One of the best ways to learn is to teach. Could you coach other people to achieve their own financial freedom? You might think you don't have enough experience, but no one ever quite knows enough. Experts are constantly learning and gaining new knowledge and they teach and mentor others while doing this.

It doesn't matter what name you give it – coaching, teaching, mentoring, sharing or supporting – sharing what you have learned is a combination of listening, questioning and advising. It is the act of helping someone to:

- avoid the mistakes you've made with your money
- learn the shortcuts you've picked up along the way
- adopt the necessary mindset and attitude
- share their own financial needs, expectations and challenges
- regain confidence when they've made financial losses.

Passing this onto others is a win–win process. Those you help are better equipped to handle and grow their finances and you will gain in at least three ways:

- You will feel good about giving back.
- You will learn and grow as you reflect on your own financial journey.
- New flashes of inspiration will come to you as you share your experiences.

Are you ready to start giving back through teaching and mentoring others?

95

Put it into action

Help your 'financial partners'

You might be jointly growing your wealth with a spouse or partner, building up a business with an ex-colleague, jointly investing with friends in property or in something unusual like a wine club. All these people are your financial partners and it's important that they're as knowledge-able and financially aware as you. Teach them what you know and be open to learning from them, mutually mentoring and supporting each other.

Teach young people

Most parents never teach their children about money and finance. What a missed opportunity. Start today and help them lose their naivety about finance so that they can avoid some of the mistakes others make in their teens and early adulthood.

Teach the community

I have a friend who volunteers her time at a local women's prison, teaching the prisoners about making money. Her most recent workshops focused on starting a business and reducing debts. How could you help people in your community?

NO NEED TO SPRINT, IT'S A MARATHON

'Investing is all about watching the trees grow, a tall skyscraper being built and the seasons passing.'

In a 2017 mega study entitled 'The Rate of Return on Everything, 1870–2015', a group of economists from Germany and the US analysed the annual rates of return of government bonds, equities and residential property. They reviewed the data for 16 countries, including the US, Germany, Japan and the UK, and calculated that the average rates of return (adjusted for inflation) over the 145-year period were:

Housing	7.05%
Equities	6.89%
Bonds	2.5%
Treasury Bills	0.98%

If your relatives had invested £1,000 in 1870 in a mix of housing and equities, you would have inherited about £18 million today. This is an extreme example of investing for the long term, a strategy referred to as 'buying and holding'.

All the evidence suggests that the longer you hold an investment, the more assured you are of a positive annual return.

The Schwab Center for Financial Research analysed the returns of the S&P 500 index over 85 years from 1926–2011. They found that to be 100% assured of a positive average annual return, you would have to have held an investment in the index for 20 years (at any point during this 85-year period). They calculated this would have given a return of between 3-17%. Holding for a shorter period risked you experiencing very large losses, e.g. holding for any three-year period would have given you annual returns of between –27% to –31%. In other words, you could have lost a third of your investment or could have made that much. Sounds like a visit to a casino!

These historical analyses point to one conclusion: investment is not a short-term activity. If you are looking for quick victories, be prepared for a quick defeat. Having a long-term orientation can assure you of financial success.

Take time to build up wealth.

Put it into action

Let go and be patient

Try dividing your assets or funds into two parts.

- *Actively managed*: this is the portion you want to actively work with, adjusting through buying and selling as markets move.
- *'Buy and hold'*: this is the portion you want to simply leave to grow. This part of your portfolio should rise as a percentage of your entire wealth as you get older.

A 'buy and hold' strategy

These historical studies support the strategy of dollar-cost averaging: the idea of investing the same amounts each month or year into the same funds and never cutting your losses when the market falls.

Keep your eyes open

There are suggestions that buying and holding quality companies in S&P index types is no longer a sure bet. In part this reflects the extreme disruption impacting many established Fortune 500 companies.

Just as we were once used to putting our cash into high interest savings accounts, sitting back and living off the returns, only for those times to end as interest rates fell close to zero, it could be that the long term-focused buying and holding of equities might no longer be as sure a bet as it used to be. This is something for you to be aware of and consider as you plan your investments.

SLEEP PEACEFULLY AT NIGHT

'If you leave your front door open, don't be surprised when someone pops in and helps themselves to your stuff.'

There's nothing worse than losing money simply because you didn't protect what you had. Imagine buying your dream home only for it to flood or burn down, and then discovering that you have to pay out of your own pocket to re-build it because you hadn't taken out house insurance. Or losing your partner only to discover that the life insurance coverage had lapsed a few years earlier.

There is a range of ways you can protect different assets and investments. None can protect you 100% from all possibilities, such as stupid investments, throwing money into a start-up run by someone who has never had any business success, or lending money to someone who subsequently disappears. But it is important to think about ways of protecting yourself, to avoid facing greater losses.

Put it into action

Here are some of the essential 'protection' options for you to consider.

Protect your mortgage

In many countries, you can take out insurance on your house loan so that if you die or become incapacitated, the mortgage is paid off in part or in full. In some countries it's required by the bank giving you the mortgage. In the UK this kind of insurance is called mortgage payment protection insurance. It would typically cover your mortgage payments for two years or two-thirds of your monthly income, whichever is lower. They start paying out one or two months after you're unable to work.

Place your life insurance in a trust

Take out life insurance if you have any dependants or anyone you care about who would struggle financially if you were to die or have a serious accident. In the UK, the payout can avoid inheritance tax if the life insurance is held in a trust.

Hedging

Hedging is a form of insurance where you hold a share, raw material or a particular currency. You hold it because you expect the price to rise or because you need it for your business. If you worry about a price fall you can buy what is called a put option. This is an example of a derivative, which allows you to make money when the share, currency or other product falls in value. This gain would offset the loss you would make from your actual holdings of that asset.

Key man and business insurance

There are all kinds of insurance policies available that may pay out in the event that you can't work, run your business or if your business struggles.

Deposit with protected banks

In the UK, up to £85,000 (or £170,000 for joint accounts) held in a bank or building society is protected by the Financial Services Compensation Scheme. This means that as long as your bank is part of the scheme, you would have your balances, up to these amounts, reimbursed to you in the event of the bank's closure. In the US, comparable deposit insurance is provided by the Federal Deposit Insurance Corporation. Similar schemes exist in other countries.

Do take expert advice about protecting yourself. Learn more at websites such as www.money-adviceservice.org.uk. In the US visit: www.fdic.gov.

PLAN FOR THE END

'Estate planning is the most important present you can ever give your family.'

According to a 2017 UK survey by unbiased.co.uk, only 40% of people have a will, falling to 16% for 18–34-year-olds and to 28% for 35–54-year-olds. The majority of those surveyed said they'd make a will when they are older, citing having few assets as a main reason for not doing so yet. And another startling thought: in countries where governments tax you on the wealth you leave when you die, a large proportion of your wealth ends up as tax.

So why meticulously plan how you're going to make your wealth if you don't care what happens to it after you die? You have the opportunity to specify who's going to get it and not only that but to legally minimize how much tax you pay on it.

Dying without a will (known as intestate) is not an issue if you are happy with the distribution of your wealth according to the law. A UK court would pass your wealth to your married partner and children; two-thirds to your husband or wife, and the remainder split amongst your offspring. But what if you didn't want to divide your estate in this way? What if you wanted one of your children to inherit all of your business which they'd been helping you to run or you wanted to leave a large part of your estate to a charity or another relative?

And what about helping your family minimize inheritance tax payable upon your death, by being aware of the inheritance rules, tax-free allowances, and ways of gifting your wealth to others while you're still alive?

Planning ahead will give you peace of mind now, and avoid heartache and difficulties for your family.

Put it into action

Write a will

Make sure you're one of the 40% who's made the effort to write a will, and even better, keep it updated and amend it or write a new one when needed. You don't want to leave cash to someone who died 20 years ago. Creating a will can be done cheaply or even at no cost, and there's plenty of advice available online.

Don't miss out on available allowances

Take full advantage of all the allowances available to you and use the rules to help you. For example, in the UK there's the residence nil rate band available when a home is left to direct descendants, meaning you can leave more of your wealth without them being liable for so much inheritance tax. Speak to a tax expert to familiarize yourself with all the regulations.

Gift while still alive

In the UK and other countries, there are various ways of giving to others tax-free while you're still alive such as:

- giving up to £3,000 per recipient per year (but bear in mind that if you live on for less than seven years after making any gift, it may not be totally free of inheritance tax)
- donating unlimited gifts out of surplus income (bear in mind that you may need an accountant to help you calculate what your surplus income is).

Wherever you live, one thing is for sure, the rules are complicated and far from intuitive, so get help.

Share advice with older relatives

Why not share this chapter's tips with your parents and grandparents and encourage them to plan ahead so that they don't leave all of their wealth liable to inheritance tax?

BE READY TO LIVE BEYOND 100

'We talk about starting a second life after 50. I think we actually live more than two.'

The UN estimates that there will be 3.7 million centenarians by 2050, compared with half a million today. In fact, there's a 20% chance you will live beyond 100 according to a UK Office for National Statistics study which also forecasts that by 2081 there will be over 650,000 centenarians in the UK, a large increase from today's 15,000.

The world's oldest person to date, Jeanne Calment, died at the age of 122 and according to researchers at the University of Groningen, living to well in excess of 100 could become quite common. They estimate that by 2070, one in 20,000 of us will live beyond 125. This means it's possible you could spend more years in retirement than you did working and studying.

Retirement age	Approx. years of working life	Approx. years in retirement[1]	Approx. years in retirement[2]
50	30	50	70
60	40	40	60
70	50	30	50
([1] Assumes dying at 100; [2] Assumes dying at 120)			

Increasing numbers of retirees are not simply living quietly off a pension. They're travelling and living in other parts of the world, taking up new hobbies and activities, running businesses and starting new ones, working and doing charity and voluntary work.

How do you plan financially for this?

Put it into action

Retirement is dead, long live working

What does the future hold? It looks like many of us will choose not to formally retire but to carry on in our existing jobs or explore new career and business opportunities.

London Business School academics Andrew Scott and Lynda Gratton calculate that if you live beyond 100 and save 10% of your salary every year, you will need to work into your late 80s to enable you to live off a pension and savings equal to half of your previous salary. In many countries state pensions are quite low which further increases the need to keep on working.

So unless you've built up sufficient wealth, you'll be working well into your 70s and beyond. According to the UK's Department for Work and Pensions one in ten of the over-70s are still working to remain both physically and mentally challenged as well as for financial reasons.

Living beyond 100 is a gift and with medical advances, you can hope to be healthy for most of your later years as well. So keep building up your investment portfolio but perhaps make it a little more conservative than in your earlier years, start a business, or take a new job so you don't eat into your savings.

WAS IT ALL WORTH IT?

'Looking back, only have small regrets. The kind you can spend a few minutes putting right.'

In years to come, what will you regret doing, or not doing, today? The Australian hospice nurse Bronnie Ware interviewed hundreds of dying patients and heard the same things repeated again and again:

- I wish I'd had the courage to live a life true to myself, not the life others expected of me.
- I wish I hadn't worked so hard.
- I wish I'd had the courage to express my feelings.
- I wish I'd stayed in touch with my friends.
- I wish that I'd let myself be happier.

While you're busy investing your time and energy in achieving your financial goals, don't forget to look around you and appreciate what you've got.

> Getting rich isn't actually all that important at the end of the day. That's what people about to die will tell you.

Put it into action

Don't lose things that money can't buy

Starting today, stop regretting things in your past or in your present. Stop feeling upset and carrying a bad conscience. Do what you need to do today, so that when your time comes you're at peace with all of your choices and decisions. Keeping a journal is a great way to stay in touch with your decisions and plans, making sure that regrets never materialise. Focus in particular on these three areas:

1. Time and dreams

Are you using your time well or do you need to spend it differently? What activities do you cut back or make time for, even if they're not income generating?

2. Family and relationships

Who do you want to spend more time with and who needs less of your time? How do you need to change the quality of the time spent with those closest to you?

3. Apologies and recognition

Is there anyone you need to apologize to? Saying sorry is a powerful, cleansing experience.

And finally, is there anyone you need to say thank you to? Sometimes the people closest to you are the ones you overlook.

No one can create an amazing life full of richness and happiness alone.

AND FINALLY ...

'It's over to you.'

I hope the ideas, exercises and suggestions in this book inspire you to action and equip you with the tools to succeed on your financial journey.

Build on the 100 things listed here. Do your own discovering, learning, experimenting. Create a list that works for you.

I would love to keep in touch to hear how you're succeeding in becoming wealthier, both financially and in creating a more fulfilling and meaningful life. Please connect with me on Facebook, LinkedIn, Twitter or Instagram. Email me at nigel@silkroadpartnership.com.

REFERENCES

Chapter 3

Charles Schwab & Co., Inc., Modern Wealth Index, https://content.schwab.com/web/retail/public/about-schwab/schwab-modern-wealth-index-2018.pdf (accessed May 2019)

Emolument.com, How much do you need to feel wealthy? https://mailchi.mp/emolument/press-release-which-jobs-are-most-likely-to-cause-burn-outs-647429 (accessed May 2019)

Chapter 5

Legg Mason Global Asset Management, Rise of the conviction investor, https://www.leqqmason.com/content/dam/legg-mason/documents/en/insights-and-education/brochure/global-investment-survey-brochure.pdf (accessed May 2019)

Chapter 7

Andrew T. Jebb, Louis Tay, Ed Diener and Shigehiro Oishi, Happiness, income satiation and turning points around the world, https://www.nature.com/articles/s41562-017-0277-0 (accessed May 2019)

Chapter 9

Gallup's Annual Economy and Personal Finance survey, Dennis Jacobe, One in three Americans prepare a detailed household budget, https://news.gallup.com/poll/162872/one-three-americans-prepare-detailed-household-budget.aspx (accessed May 2019)

Office for National Statistics, Making ends meet: are households living beyond their means? https://www.ons.gov.uk/economy/nationalaccounts/uksectoraccounts/articles/makingendsmeetarehouseholdslivingbeyondtheirmeans/2018-07-26 (accessed May 2019)

Chapter 10

Business Wire, Fidelity® Survey Finds 86 Percent of Millionaires Are Self-Made, https://www.businesswire.com/news/home/20120719005724/en/Fidelity%C2%AE-Survey-Finds-86-Percent-Millionaires-Self-Made (accessed May 2019)

Dr Nolen-Hoeksema, https://www.nytimes.com/2013/01/14/us/susan-nolen-hoeksema-psychologist-who-studied-depression-in-women-dies-at-53.html. Various studies including: https://www.ncbi.nlm.nih.gov/pmc/articles/PMC3398979/ (accessed May 2019)

Dwayne Johnson – official Twitter account, https://twitter.com/therock/status/1470165687804
96897?lang=en (accessed May 2019)

Chapter 12

Catherine T. Shea, Low on self-control? Surrounding yourself with strong-willed friends may
help, *Psychological Science*, https://www.psychologicalscience.org/news/releases/low-on-self-
control-surrounding-yourself-with-strong-willed-friends-may-help.html (accessed May 2019)

Chapter 14

Taylor Tepper/Bankrate.com, Most Americans have inadequate savings, but they aren't sweating it,
https://www.bankrate.com/banking/savings/financial-security-june-2018/ (accessed May 2019)

Emma Elsworthy, A quarter of British adults have no savings, study reveals, *Independent*, https://
www.independent.co.uk/news/uk/home-news/british-adults-savings-none-quarter-debt-cost-
living-emergencies-survey-results-a8265111.html (accessed May 2019)

Financial Conduct Authority, Understanding the financial lives of UK adults: Findings from the
FCA's Financial Lives, Survey 2017, https://www.fca.org.uk/publication/research/financial-lives-
survey-2017.pdf (accessed May 2019)

Chapter 17

Miles Brignall, Survey reveals 6m Britons fear never being debt-free with 25% struggling to
make ends meet and 62% worried about personal debt levels, https://www.theguardian.com/
money/2017/oct/30/average-uk-debt-at-8000-per-person-not-including-the-mortgage (accessed May 2019)

Matt Tatham/Experian Information Services, Inc., A look at US consumer credit card debt,
https://www.experian.com/blogs/ask-experian/state-of-credit-cards/ (accessed May 2019)

Chapter 20

Dalton Conley, https://www.neatorama.com/2008/09/05/rich-people-work-longer-hours-than-
poor-people-do/ and https://www.nytimes.com/2008/09/02/opinion/02conley.html (accessed
May 2019)

Daniel Kahneman and Angus Deaton, High income improves evaluation of life but not emotional well-being, https://www.princeton.edu/~deaton/downloads/deaton_kahneman_high_in-
come_improves_evaluation_August2010.pdf (accessed May 2019)

Mihaly Csikszentmihalyi, see https://en.wikipedia.org/wiki/Mihaly_Csikszentmihalyi (accessed May 2019)

Chapter 25

Credit Suisse, Global Wealth Report 2018, https://www.credit-suisse.com/corporate/en/research/research-institute/global-wealth-report.html (accessed May 2019)

One in three pensioners living well below the poverty line, says report, *The Guardian*, https://www.theguardian.com/australia-news/2016/sep/15/one-in-three-pensioners-living-well-below-the-poverty-line-says-report (accessed May 2019)

Ekaterina Bystrova, Syndicate Room/FTI Consulting, https://www.syndicateroom.com/learn/investor-tools-reports/big-investor-survey-2018 (accessed May 2019)

Chapter 27

Soyoung Q. Park, Thorsten Kahnt, Azade Dogan, Sabrina Strang, Ernst Fehr and Philippe N. Tobler, *Nature Communications*, A neural link between generosity and happiness, https://www.nature.com/articles/ncomms15964 (accessed May 2019)

Brent Simpson (University of South Carolina) and Robb Willer (University of California, Berkeley), Altruism and indirect reciprocity: the interaction of person and situation in prosocial behaviour, https://greatergood.berkeley.edu/images/uploads/Simpson-AltruismReciprocity.pdf (accessed May 2019)

Chapter 31

Thomas C. Corley, I spent 5 years studying poor people and here are 4 destructive money habits they had, http://richhabits.net/i-spent-5-years-studying-poor-people-and-here-are-4-destructive-money-habits-they-had/ (accessed May 2019)

Chapter 33

Eugene O'Kelly (Afterword by Corinne O'Kelly), *Customers who Viewed Chasing Daylight: How My Forthcoming Death Transformed My Life* (first edition), USA: McGraw-Hill Education (15 October 2007)

Chapter 39

Chris Taylor, Reuters, 70% of rich families lose their wealth by the second generation, http://money.com/money/3925308/rich-families-lose-wealth/ (accessed May 2019)

US Trust Insights on Wealth and Worth (2015), https://newsroom.bankofamerica.com/press-releases/global-wealth-and-investment-management/us-trust-study-high-net-worth-investors (accessed May 2019)

Chapter 42

Himalayan Database, https://www.himalayandatabase.com/ (accessed May 2019)

Chapter 43

The Luck Factor, Richard Wiseman (Miramax, 2003)

Chapter 46

Details of study can be found at https://www.aaii.com/journal/article/trading-more-frequently-leads-to-worse-returns (accessed May 2019), which quotes from Brad M. Barber and Terrance Odean, 'Trading is hazardous to your wealth: the common stock investment performance of individual investors', *The Journal of Finance*, Volume LV, Number 2, April 2000. © John Wiley & Sons.

Chapter 48

Amy J. C. Cuddy, S. Jack Schultz, Nathan E. Fosse, P-Curving a more comprehensive body of research on postural feedback reveals clear evidential value for power-posing effects: reply to Simmons and Simonsohn (2017) *Psychological Science*, https://journals.sagepub.com/eprint/CzbNAn7Ch6ZZirK9yMGH/full

Michael W. Kraus and Dacher Keltner, Rich man, poor man: study shows body language can indicate socioeconomic status, https://www.psychologicalscience.org/news/releases/rich-man-poor-man-study-shows-body-language-can-indicate-socioeconomic-status.html (accessed May 2019)

Spencer D. Kelly, Sarah Ward, Peter Creigh and James Bartolotti, An intentional stance modulates the integration of gesture and speech during comprehension, *Brain and Language*, http://www.colgate.edu/portaldata/imagegallery/faculty/90382552/imagegallery/faculty/Kelly,%20Creigh%20and%20Bartolotti%202007.pdf (accessed May 2019)

Janine Willis and Alexander Todorov, First impressions: making up your mind after a 100-ms exposure to a face, https://www.princeton.edu/news/2006/08/22/snap-judgments-decide-faces-character-psychologist-finds (accessed May 2019)

G.L. Stewart, S.L. Dustin, M.R. Barrick and T.C. Darnold, Exploring the handshake in employment interviews, *Journal of Applied Psychology* (September 2008), https://www.ncbi.nlm.nih.gov/pubmed/18808231 (accessed May 2019)

Careerbuilder.com (2010) http://www.careerbuilder.com/share/aboutus/pressreleasesdetail.aspx?sd=7%2F29%2F2010&id=pr581&ed=12%2F31%2F2010 (accessed May 2019)

Chapter 52

Jonah Berger (University of Pennsylvania), *Contagious: Why Things Catch* (Simon & Schuster, 2013)

Chapter 53

How the 0.001% invest, *The Economist* (15 December 2018), https://www.economist.com/leaders/2018/12/15/how-the-0001-invest (accessed May 2019)

Chapter 56

Bill Gates interview with *Time* (2017), http://time.com/4786837/bill-gates-books-reading/ (accessed May 2019)

Richard Branson blog (15 December 2017), https://www.virgin.com/richard-branson/read-lead-0 (accessed May 2019)

Pew Research Center, The rising cost of not going to college, https://www.pewsocialtrends.org/2014/02/11/the-rising-cost-of-not-going-to-college/ (accessed: May 2019)

Department of Education, UK, Graduate labour market statistics (2016), https://assets.publishing.service.gov.uk/government/uploads/system/uploads/attachment_data/file/610805/GLMS_2016_v2.pdf (accessed May 2019)

Chapter 60

Accenture (2015), https://newsroom.accenture.com/industries/global-media-industry-analyst-relations/accenture-research-finds-listening-more-difficult-in-todays-digital-workplace.htm (accessed May 2019)

Ralph G. Nichols (University of Minnesota) and Leonard A. Stevens, Listening to people, *Harvard Business Review*, https://hbr.org/1957/09/listening-to-people (accessed May 2019)

Chapter 61

Jeremy Kahn and Martijn Van Der Starre, Google lowered 2015 taxes by $3.6 billion using 'Dutch Sandwich', Bloomberg, https://www.bloomberg.com/news/articles/2016-12-21/google-lowered-2015-taxes-by-3-6-billion-using-dutch-sandwich (accessed May 2019)

Chapter 62

United States Census Bureau, Income and Poverty in the United States: 2017, https://www.census.gov/library/publications/2018/demo/p60-263.html (accessed May 2019)

Chapter 63

Bill Gates video interview at *The David Rubenstein Show: Bill Gates* (17 October 2016), https://www.bloomberg.com/news/videos/2016-10-17/the-david-rubenstein-show-bill-gates. Referenced online e.g. at: https://www.businessinsider.com/bill-gates-splurge-porsche-911-microsoft-money-2016-10?r=US&IR=T (accessed May 2019)

Warrant Buffett quote, https://www.goodreads.com/quotes/7374480-if-you-buy-things-you-do-not-need-soon-you (accessed May 2019)

Chapter 65

Barbara L Fredrickson, The broaden–and–build theory of positive emotions, The Royal Society (September 2019), https://www.ncbi.nlm.nih.gov/pmc/articles/PMC1693418/ (accessed May 2019)

Martin E. Seligman and Peter Schulman, Explanatory style as a predictor of productivity and quitting among life insurance sales agents, *Journal of Personality and Social Psychology* (April 1986), https://www.researchgate.net/publication/232497771_Explanatory_Style_as_a_Predictor_of_Productivity_and_Quitting_Among_Life_Insurance_Sales_Agents (accessed May 2019)

Gabrielle Oettingen quote from https://www.cnbc.com/2017/10/05/why-should-you-be-highly-optimistic-if-you-want-to-be-successful.html (accessed May 2019)

Chapter 66

Benjamin Graham, *The Intelligent Investor: The Definitive Book on Value Investing* (Collins Business Essentials, 2006)

Julian Wadley, The improvements that add value to your house (July 2017), https://blog.zopa.com/2017/07/18/improvements-that-add-value-to-your-house/ (accessed May 2019)

Chapter 67

MBO Partners, State of Independence, https://www.mbopartners.com/wp-content/uploads/2019/02/State_of_Independence_2018.pdf (accessed: May 2019)

Maximilian Yoshioka, How entrepreneurial was the UK in 2015?, Centre for Entrepreneurs (January 2016), https://centreforentrepreneurs.org/how-entrepreneurial-was-the-uk-in-2015/ (accessed May 2019)

Department for Business, Energy and Industrial Strategy. Business population estimates for the UK and regions 2018 (October 2018), https://assets.publishing.service.gov.uk/government/uploads/system/uploads/attachment_data/file/746599/OFFICIAL_SENSITIVE_-_BPE_2018_-_statistical_release_FINAL_FINAL.pdf (accessed May 2019)

Kristin Pryor, Here are the startup failure rates by industry, https://tech.co/news/startup-failure-rates-industry-2016-01 (accessed May 2019)

Chapter 68

Internet statistics available at https://www.internetworldstats.com/stats.htm (numbers keep changing real time) (accessed May 2019)

Simon Kemp, Digital in 2018: world's internet users pass the 4 billion mark, https://wearesocial.com/blog/2018/01/global-digital-report-2018 (accessed May 2019)

Chapter 71

Amy Guttman, A successful VC and founder says intuition is everything, *Forbes*, https://www.forbes.com/sites/amyguttman/2015/09/28/a-successful-vc-and-founder-says-intuition-is-everything/ (accessed May 2019)

Chapter 72

Brad M. Barber (University of California, Davis) and Terrance Odean (University of California, Berkeley - Haas School of Business), The behavior of individual investors (7 September 2011), https://papers.ssrn.com/sol3/papers.cfm?abstract_id=1872211 (accessed May 2019)

Chapter 74

Ho Law, Sara Ireland and Zulfi Hussain, *The Psychology of Coaching, Mentoring and Learning* (first edition) (Wiley, 2007)

Credit Suisse, Global Wealth Report 2018, https://www.credit-suisse.com/corporate/en/research/research-institute/global-wealth-report.html (accessed May 2019)

Chapter 75

Russel Kinnel, Mind the gap: why investors lag funds, *Morningstar* (February 2013), https://www.morningstar.com/articles/582626/mind-the-gap-why-investors-lag-funds.html (accessed May 2019)

John Authers, Investor returns are all about the timing, *Financial Times*, https://www.ft.com/content/338eea6c-e8db-11e4-b7e8-00144feab7de (accessed May 2019)

Fund managers rarely outperform the market for long, *The Economist*, https://www.economist.com/finance-and-economics/2017/06/24/fund-managers-rarely-outperform-the-market-for-long (accessed May 2019)

Chapter 76

7 bad habits truly wealthy people never have, https://www.inc.com/quora/7-bad-habits-truly-wealthy-people-never-have.html (accessed May 2019)

Statista data: (US) https://www.statista.com/statistics/186833/average-television-use-per-person-in-the-us-since-2002/; (UK) https://www.statista.com/statistics/528255/uk-survey-hours-spent-watching-tv-weekly/ (accessed May 2019)

T.S. Conner, K.L. Brookie, A.C. Richardson and M.A. Polak, On carrots and curiosity: eating fruit and vegetables is associated with greater flourishing in daily life, *British Journal of Health Psychology* (May 2015), https://www.ncbi.nlm.nih.gov/pubmed/25080035 (accessed May 2019)

Candice L. Hogan, Jutta Mata and Laura L. Carstensen, Exercise holds immediate benefits for affect and cognition in younger and older adults, *Psychology and Aging* (June 2013) https://www.ncbi.nlm.nih.gov/pmc/articles/PMC3768113/ (accessed May 2019)

Chapter 77

L. Ganzini, B.H. McFarland and D. Cutler, Prevalence of mental disorders after catastrophic financial loss, *Journal of Nervous and Mental Disease* (November 1990), https://www.ncbi.nlm.nih.gov/pubmed/2230754 (accessed May 2019)

Melissa McInerney, Jennifer M. Mellor and Lauren Hersch Nicholas, Recession depression: mental health effects of the 2008 stock market crash, *Journal of Health Economics* (December 2013) https://www.ncbi.nlm.nih.gov/pmc/articles/PMC3874451/ (accessed May 2019)

Chapter 79

Syndicate Room, The big investor survey 2018, https://www.syndicateroom.com/learn/investor-tools-reports/big-investor-survey-2018 (accessed May 2019)

Asset Allocation Survey, https://www.aaii.com/assetallocationsurvey (Numbers change in this real-time survey at this site)

Chapter 80

Daniel C. Molden and Chin Ming Hui (Northwestern University), Promoting de-escalation of commitment: a regulatory-focus perspective on sunk costs (2011), https://www.psychology.northwestern.edu/documents/faculty-publications/molden-%20hui_2011.pdf (accessed May 2019)

Chapter 81

Morgan Stanley, 84% of Millennial investors interested in sustainable investing, https://sustaincase.com/morgan-stanley-84-of-millennial-investors-interested-in-sustainable-investing/ (accessed May 2019)

UBS Investor Watch, *Global insights: What's on investors' minds?* Volume 2 (2018), https://www.ubs.com/content/dam/ubs/microsites/ubs-investor-watch/IW-09-2018/return-on-value-global-report-final.pdf (accessed May 2019)

Schroders Institutional, Investor Study 2018, Institutional perspectives on sustainable investing, https://www.schroders.com/en/sysglobalassets/schroders_institutional_investor_study_sustainability_report_2018.pdf (accessed May 2019)

Mark Haefele, Sustainable investing can propel long-term returns (September 2018), https://www.ft.com/content/292ecaa7-294c-3a4b-bde6-a7a744cb85a9 (accessed May 2019)

Sarah Moore, Fit for the future: how ethical investing went mainstream, *Money Week* (15 February 2018), https://moneyweek.com/481615/sri-esg-how-ethical-and-sustainable-investing-went-mainstream/ (accessed: May 2019)

Chapter 82

Pierre Azoulay (MIT and NBER), Benjamin F. Jones (Northwestern University and NBER), J. Daniel Kim (MIT) and Javier Miranda (US Census Bureau), Age and high-growth entrepreneurship (23 March 2018), https://www.kellogg.northwestern.edu/faculty/jones-ben/htm/Age%20and%20 High%20Growth%20Entrepreneurship.pdf (accessed May 2019)

Chapter 83

6 million UK households could not survive until the weekend on savings according to First Direct, Social Media Newsroom (9 January 2012), https://www.newsroom.firstdirect.com/press/ release/6_million_uk_households_could (accessed: May 2019)

Chapter 85

Marc Alpert and Howard Raiffa (1982) A progress report on the training of probability assessors. In Daniel Kahneman, Paul Slovic, Amos Tversky *Judgment Under Uncertainty: Heuristics and Biases* (Cambridge University Press, 1982), https://philpapers.org/rec/ALPAPR (accessed: May 2019)

Stav Atir, Emily Rosenzweig and David Dunning, When knowledge knows no bounds: self-perceived expertise predicts claims of impossible knowledge, *Psychological Science* (14 July 2015), https://journals.sagepub.com/doi/abs/10.1177/0956797615588195 (accessed: May 2019)

Brad M. Barber and Terrance Odean, Boys will be boys: gender, overconfidence, and common stock investment, https://faculty.haas.berkeley.edu/odean/Papers%20current%20versions/ BoysWillBeBoys.pdf (accessed May 2019)

Daniel Kahneman, *Thinking, Fast and Slow* (Farrar, Straus and Giroux, 2013)

Brad M. Barber (University of California, Davis) and Terrance Odean (University of California, Berkeley – Haas School of Business), Trading is hazardous to your wealth: the common stock investment performance of individual investors (12 April 2000), https://papers.ssrn.com/sol3/ papers.cfm?abstract_id=219228 (accessed May 2019)

Alicia R. Williams and S. Kathi Brown, 2017 Retirement Confidence Survey, AARP Research (December 2017), https://www.aarp.org/content/dam/aarp/research/surveys_statistics/econ/2017/2017-re-tirement-confidence.doi.10.26419%252Fres.00174.001.pdf (accessed May 2019)

James Montier, Behaving badly, Global Equity Strategy, DrKW Macro research (February 2006), https://www.kellogg.northwestern.edu/faculty/weber/decs-452/behaving_badly.pdf (accessed May 2019)

Chapter 87

Adam Bryant, *The Corner Office: Indispensable and Unexpected Lessons from CEOs on How to Lead and Succeed* (first edition), (Times Books, 2011)

Francesca Gino, The business case for curiosity, *Harvard Business Review*, https://hbr.org/2018/09/curiosity (accessed May 2019)

Paul Carrick Brunson, I've worked for two billionaires. Here's what I learned from them (18 March 2016), https://www.linkedin.com/pulse/ive-worked-two-billionaires-heres-what-i-learned-from-brunson/ (accessed May 2019)

Legg Mason Global Asset Management, Legg Mason Global Investment Survey (2018), https://www.leggmason.com/content/dam/legg-mason/documents/en/insights-and-education/brochure/global-investment-survey-brochure.pdf (accessed May 2019)

Jamie Ballard, 79% of Americans are familiar with at least one kind of cryptocurrency, YouGov (September 2018), https://today.yougov.com/topics/technology/articles-reports/2018/09/06/cryptocurrency-bitcoin-popular-americans (accessed May 2019)

Chapter 89

Roger Fisher, William L. Ury and Bruce Patton, *Getting to Yes: Negotiating Agreement Without Giving In* (Penguin Books, 1991)

Chapter 90

Emotional Intelligence Can Boost Your Career And Save Your Life, TalentSmart, https://www.talentsmart.com/articles/Emotional-Intelligence-Can-Boost-Your-Career-And-Save-Your-Life-915340665-p-1.html (accessed May 2019)

Gregory J. Feist (San Jose State University) and Frank X Barron, Predicting creativity from early to late adulthood: Intellect, potential, and personality, *Journal of Research in Personality* 37(2):62–88 (April 2003), https://www.researchgate.net/publication/222085214_Predicting_creativity_from_early_to_late_adulthood_Intellect_potential_and_personality (accessed May 2019)

Joseph C. Rode (Miami University), Marne L. Arthaud-Day (Kansas State University), Aarti Ramaswami (École Supérieure des Sciences Economiques et Commerciales) and Satoris Howes, A time-lagged study of emotional intelligence and salary, *Journal of Vocational Behavior* 101 (May 2017), https://www.researchgate.net/publication/316816644_A_time-lagged_study_of_emotional_intelligence_and_salary (accessed May 2019)

Chapter 91

S. McMains and S. Kastner, Interactions of top-down and bottom-up mechanisms in human visual cortex, *Journal of Neuroscience* (January 2011), https://www.ncbi.nlm.nih.gov/pubmed/21228167 (accessed May 2019)

Chapter 96

Oscar Jord, Katharina Knoll, Dmitry Kuvshinov, Moritz Schularick and Alan M. Taylor The Rate of Return on Everything, 1870–2015 (March 2019), https://economics.harvard.edu/files/economics/files/ms28533.pdf (accessed May 2019)

The Schwab Center for Financial Research, http://retirementdesk.com/wp-content/uploads/schwab-charts-through-06302011.pdf (accessed May 2019)

Chapter 98

31 million UK adults at risk of dying without a will, unbiased (2 October 2017) https://business.unbiased.co.uk/press-releases/31-million-uk-adults-at-risk-of-dying-without-a-will-2-10-2017 (accessed May 2019)

Chapter 99

Renee Stepler, World's centenarian population projected to grow eightfold by 2050, Pew Research Center, https://www.pewresearch.org/fact-tank/2016/04/21/worlds-centenarian-population-projected-to-grow-eightfold-by-2050/ (accessed May 2019)

Office for National Statistics, What are your chances of living to 100? (14 January 2016) https://www.ons.gov.uk/peoplepopulationandcommunity/birthsdeathsandmarriages/lifeexpectancies/articles/whatareyourchancesoflivingto100/2016-01-14 (accessed May 2019)

Joop de Beer, Anastasios Bardoutsos and Fanny Janssen, Maximum human lifespan may increase to 125 years, *Nature*, 546: E16–E17 (29 June 2017) https://www.nature.com/articles/nature22792?draft=collection&platform=oscar (accessed May 2019)

Chapter 100

Bronnie Ware, *The Top Five Regrets of the Dying: A Life Transformed by the Dearly Departing* (Hay House, 2012)